W9-CPE-457

WITHDRAWN

ISSUES THAT CONCERN YOU

Teen Parenting

Laurie Willis, *Book Editor*

GREENHAVEN PRESS

A part of Gale, Cengage Learning

GALE
CENGAGE Learning·

Detroit • New York • San Francisco • New Haven, Conn • Waterville, Maine • London

Elizabeth Des Chenes, *Managing Editor*

© 2012 Greenhaven Press, a part of Gale, Cengage Learning

Gale and Greenhaven Press are registered trademarks used herein under license.

For more information, contact:
Greenhaven Press
27500 Drake Rd.
Farmington Hills, MI 48331-3535
Or you can visit our Internet site at gale.cengage.com

For product information and technology assistance, contact us at

Gale Customer Support, 1-800-877-4253
For permission to use material from this text or product, submit all requests online at www.cengage.com/permissions

Further permissions questions can be e-mailed to permissionrequest@cengage.com

Articles in Greenhaven Press anthologies are often edited for length to meet page requirements. In addition, original titles of these works are changed to clearly present the main thesis and to explicitly indicate the author's opinion. Every effort is made to ensure that Greenhaven Press accurately reflects the original intent of the authors. Every effort has been made to trace the owners of copyrighted material.

Cover image © Mika/Comet/Corbis

LIBRARY OF CONGRESS CATALOGING-IN-PUBLICATION DATA
Teen parenting / Laurie Willis, book editor.
p. cm. -- (Issues that concern you)
Includes bibliographical references and index.
ISBN 978-0-7377-5700-2 (hardcover)
1. Teenage parents. 2. Teenage pregnancy. I. Willis, Laurie.
HQ759.64.T417 2012
306.85'6--dc23
2011027147

Printed in the United States of America
1 2 3 4 5 6 7 15 14 13 12 11

CONTENTS

"I got to go back to school . . . to get a good job . . . but don't know when. . . . I live with my mom. . . . I have to get a job, when the baby is older . . . so I can someday move out."

The above quote is from a teen mother who was interviewed as part of a study by Josephine DeVito that was reported in the *Journal of Perinatal Education*. The quote captures the sentiments of many teen moms. Although they may have a desire to finish school and get a better job, they have no specific plans to actually do so. The immediate needs of caring for a child take precedence, and they are not able to focus their energies on their own development.

A fact sheet by Child Trends gives the statistics:

Slightly more than one-half of young women who had been teen mothers received a high school diploma by the age of 22, compared with 89 percent of young women who had not given birth during their teen years. Furthermore, results of our analyses show that young women who had a child before the age of 18 were even less likely than were those who had a child when they were 18 or 19 to earn a high school diploma before the age of 22, although the rates of GED [high school diploma equivalent] attainment in the former group were slightly higher.

Although the data is clear that there is a significant difference when comparing the high school graduation (or GED) rate for teen moms with teens who are not moms, there are varying opinions about the underlying causes. Some say that teens who become mothers were already more likely to drop out of school, due to factors unrelated to their pregnancy and childbirth. The Child Trends study quoted above reports that "many teens who become mothers lag behind in school academically and that a substantial percentage drop out *before* their pregnancy."

Others say that having a child to care for is the chief reason that so many teen mothers do not complete high school. An article on the website www.teenpregnancystatistics.org highlights some of the reasons given:

- feeling embarrassed or awkward at school
- health concerns for themselves or their children
- finding daycare or childcare
- safety fears
- lack of support
- the need to work
- not knowing her options
- being behind in school

Some schools are specifically working to help young mothers continue their education. For example, Compadre High School in Tempe, Arizona, has a Teen Aged Pregnancy and Parenting Program, which, according to an article on azcentral. com, "includes parenting classes, mentoring, free bus service, free child care and scholarships for private child care. An incentive program rewards classroom accomplishments with opportunities to shop for baby goods donated to a ministore on campus." The dropout rate at this school is only 8 percent, much lower than the national average.

School completion is just one of the many issues surrounding teen parenting. The viewpoints in this book examine some of these issues. They include the challenges of being a teen mother or father, how having teen parents affects children, how teen parents relate to their families, how teen parents are learning about the responsibilities of parenting, and how television and other media influence opinions about teen parenting. In addition, the volume contains several appendixes to help the reader understand and explore the topic, including a bibliography and a list of organizations to contact for further information. The appendix titled "What You Should Know About Teen Parenting" offers

There are many reasons teen mothers do not finish high school, among them feeling embarrassed at school, health concerns, finding affordable daycare, and lack of support.

facts and statistics. The appendix "What You Should Do About Teen Parenting" offers tips for young people grappling with an understanding of the issues. With all these features, *Issues That Concern You: Teen Parenting* provides an excellent resource for everyone interested in this increasingly important issue.

ONE

Being Teen Parents Is Challenging

Melissa Daly

> Melissa Daly is a writer based in New York City. In this viewpoint, she discusses some of the challenges faced by teen parents. These challenges include making decisions about continuing a relationship as parents of a child, dealing with money issues, finding friends who are supportive, and caring for a child as it grows from baby to toddler to teen. Daly encourages teens to consider these challenges before having sex and to consistently use contraception if they decide to be sexually active.

Baby movies such as *Knocked Up* and *Juno*, both recently red-hot at the box office, share a common thread. They give the impression that accidental pregnancy is not only trendy, but may be even good for you. In those flicks, slackers and geeks get the girl . . . after they get her pregnant.

With 17-year-old Nickelodeon star Jamie Lynn Spears giving birth this past June [2008], you might question whether having a baby now is really such a bad thing. After all, more teens are becoming parents. In 2006, the birth rate among Americans age 15 to 19 jumped for the first time since 1991.

Watch out: A casual attitude about teen parenthood can put you at higher risk of experiencing it, "There's a small minority of teens actively seeking to get pregnant, and by and large they succeed. Then there's a large group who really don't want to get pregnant, and by and large they don't," says Bill Albert, deputy director of the National Campaign to Prevent Teen and Unplanned Pregnancy.

"The problem is those in the middle," he continues, "kids who are ambivalent, who aren't trying to conceive, but don't think it would be the worst thing in the world. Studies show that these ambivalent teens get pregnant at the same rate as those who are actively trying." Here are a few factors to consider.

Having a Baby Together Doesn't Guarantee a Loving Relationship

The heroines of *Knocked Up* and *Juno* wind up in loving relationships with their babies' fathers—in fact, these movies make it seem like pregnancy was what brought them together. The reality for teens? "It's incredibly rare that the father stays in the picture more than a year or two after the birth," says Albert.

Staying involved isn't easy, as 17-year-old Josh from Marble Hill, Mo., found out after his girlfriend had their daughter last year. "We're still a couple, but things are not the best between us," he says. Because Josh lives three hours away from his girlfriend, and her parents advised her not to put Josh's name on the birth certificate, custody and visitation have become a constant struggle. "My daughter's name is Kayleigh, which is one of the few things I got a say in. Being a father at my age, they jerk the baby away from you, and you can't make the kind of money you need to get the rights to your kid."

Money problems aren't unusual for young parents. Many teens who become mothers never graduate from high school, let alone college, which greatly limits their job prospects. "I had to tend to my son all day, then at 9 or 10 p.m. start doing homework. I just couldn't put my all into it," says Leslie, 21, from the Bronx, N.Y. After having her baby at 16, Leslie joined Sistahs on the Rise, a group that fought for maternity leave for teen moms attending New York City public schools.

Teenage mothers face tough challenges concerning balancing household chores with caring for a child, finding supportive friends, and handling financial issues.

Susana, 19, found support at B.E.S.T. High School in Kirkland, Wash., an alternative school that provides on-site day care. "In the movies, they don't show how difficult it is to prepare money-wise," she says. "When I had my daughter at 16, I didn't have a job and my boyfriend didn't make enough for all of us. Sometimes we didn't have money for diapers and had to break into the piggy bank I was trying to save with."

Social Circles Not Always Supportive

Money isn't the only difficulty. Susana points out that unlike in the movies, teen parents may not have a supportive social circle. "They don't show how hard it is to tell your friends, how they talk about you afterward and start looking down on you," she says.

One of Susana's fellow students, Jasmine, agrees. Jasmine is 21 but still in high school; she found out about the B.E.S.T. program only after dropping out of her old school. "When nobody else there is pregnant, nobody understands you. Everyone stares at you. It was so hard, I stopped going." Once she had her baby, Jasmine's social life suffered. "You can't do normal things like a normal teenager," she says. "You can't watch a movie or just go hang out, because you don't have a babysitter."

Some teens see a baby as a source of unconditional love or a shortcut to adulthood, says Albert. While there may be some truth to those ideas, they tend to be shortsighted. "You can't just think about the immediate future," says Albert. "Consider also the outlying years, when the cooing little baby turns into a moody, sullen preteen girl or a mouthy adolescent boy. It's a lifetime commitment."

Jasmine can attest to that, "When they're babies, you think they're going to be like that forever—sleeping all the time, letting you hold them," she says. "But as they grow it gets harder. They start walking, talking, grabbing things. It takes a lot of patience."

Babies Also Negatively Affected by Having Teen Parents

When you think about the consequences of unprotected sex, you may focus on how parenthood would affect your life—caring for the baby 24/7 or paying child support for 18 years. But think about this: When you have a baby, the baby also has *you*. "For some young parents, the pregnancy actually gets them back on track, helps them focus," says Albert. "Unfortunately, that's not often the case for their children." Kids born to teens are more likely to grow up in poverty and become teen parents themselves.

They may also be at increased risk for complications during the pregnancy and at birth. Infants with teenage fathers are more likely to be born prematurely and have low birth weight, a recent study says. (Other research shows the same is true for infants of teenage mothers, increasing their chances of vision, hearing, and breathing problems; hyperactivity; and mental retardation.) Children of teens are also 22 percent more likely to die within their first month and 41 percent more likely to die in the first year. Those problems might be the result of young parents seeking less prenatal care, having immature reproductive systems, or having less healthy lifestyles that include smoking, drinking, or taking drugs.

Adoption Not a Popular Option

Some teen couples who have kids do stay together, finish school, and raise happy, healthy families. But they're far from the norm. Teen couples who feel the reality of raising a child is too much for them have alternatives. In *Juno*, the 16-year-old title character chooses an adoptive family for her child. Currently, only 3 percent of pregnant teenagers opt for adoption, perhaps because it's the option they know the least about or because of the heartache involved in parting from a child—something that *Juno* only scratched the surface of.

"It's an extremely difficult decision for anyone to make, regardless of how old they are," says Betsy Trondson, a social worker and birth parent/pregnancy counselor at the Children's Home Society & Family Services in St. Paul, Minn. "A lot of teens waver about their choice throughout the pregnancy. Afterward, they may feel grief and sadness, but also tremendous pride that they did what they felt was best for their baby."

Another reason adoption isn't popular: Not everyone has Juno's unconditionally supportive family.

"Adoption is more common among people in their 20s. Many teens, on the other hand, face considerable pressure to raise the child, whether from their peers or their own parents," explains Trondson.

No matter what a young couple decides when faced with an unplanned pregnancy, one thing's for sure: It won't be easy.

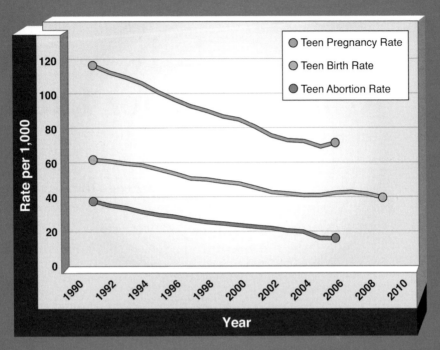

Pregnancy, Birth, and Abortion Rates Among US Females Aged 15–19 Years, 1991–2009*

- Teen Pregnancy Rate
- Teen Birth Rate
- Teen Abortion Rate

Rate per 1,000

120
100
80
60
40
20
0

1990 1992 1994 1996 1998 2000 2002 2004 2006 2008 2010

Year

*Pregnancy and abortion rates only available through 2006.

Taken from: National Center for Chronic Disease Prevention and Health Promotion, Division of Reproductive Health, "Teen Pregnancy: Improving the Lives of Young People and Strengthening Communities by Reducing Teen Pregnancy, At a Glance 2011." Centers for Disease Control and Prevention. www.cdc.gov/teenpregnancy.

Preventing conception in the first place is simpler. The only sure way to do that is not to have sex. Decide *before* the heat of the moment what you want to do so that you're prepared to stick to it. If that includes intercourse, plan what form of contraception you'll use, then follow through—every time.

"Even if you've had a lot of unprotected sex in the past and haven't conceived, that doesn't mean it won't happen the very next time," says Albert. "These are very fertile years." Learn about the different types of birth control, then choose the one (or more) you're most likely to use correctly and consistently.

TWO

Being a Teen Mother Is Particularly Challenging for Latinas

Betty Cortina

> Betty Cortina is a media consultant and the chair of The National Campaign to Prevent Teen and Unplanned Pregnancy Latino Media Advisory Group. In this viewpoint, she discusses the challenges that teen pregnancy presents to the Latino community. She points out that over half of Latina teens have babies before they are twenty, and a quarter drop out of high school. Cortina describes two schools that are addressing the issue with creative solutions. In the end, she recommends that having positive role models is the best way to convince Latina teens to pursue their own lives before they become mothers.

The news sounded good, at first. "Your cousin is having a baby," my mother declared over the phone, *"El 'shower' es el mes que viene."* ["The baby shower is next month."] I shuffled through the long list of my first, second and third cousins and wondered aloud if she was referring to this one or that one. "No," Mom says. "It's Dailene."

"Dailene?" I respond in disbelief. Dailene, you see, is in high school. She is 15. Her boyfriend is 16 and attends her same public school. They've been together since she was 14. Neither has a job. "Yes." my mother says. "And everyone is excited!" Indeed, the families of both teens had come together to plan an elegant baby shower and invited the whole family. Could I come, Mom asked?

To say I was shocked would be an understatement. How could it be that my family—the proud, hard-working family that had been stubbornly intent on the next generation doing better, on my older cousins and I going to college even though no one before us had ever gone—was now happy two of its youngest had gone down a path that would seriously challenge their future? How could it be that they were cheerily picking floral arrangements and ordering *pasteles* [a special food eaten at celebrations] for the party?

That was a little over a year ago. Dailene (whose name I've changed to protect her privacy) had her baby, has struggled through school, and had to grow up very quickly. I've been thinking about writing this article since then because I am worried about the other Dailenes out there. And because as a journalist for more than 20 years, I've seen teen pregnancy in our community grow to become a bonafide crisis.

My career started at my local newspaper in South Florida. Shortly after, I moved to Los Angeles to work for a national magazine, and a few years later headed to New York City, where I worked my way up in the industry. I've been a reporter, a writer, an editor and an editor-in-chief. I point this out not to boast, but because as I look back I realize that at every stage of my professional life the story of teen pregnancy in the Hispanic community has touched me in one way or another.

My first byline came when I was a high school intern at the local paper, for a story about a young Latina student. She was one year older than me and had just graduated, her months-old-baby in her arms. My article was about how a teen mom from my neighborhood had beaten the odds by not dropping out. I remember thinking, "Thank God that's not me."

Grim Statistics

Fast forward some 15 years, I'm working as the editor of a Hispanic women's magazine, sitting at an editorial meeting, when talk among the staff turns to a story in the newspaper about how the

Since 1995, Latina teens have had the highest teen birth rate among the major racial/ethnic groups in the United States.

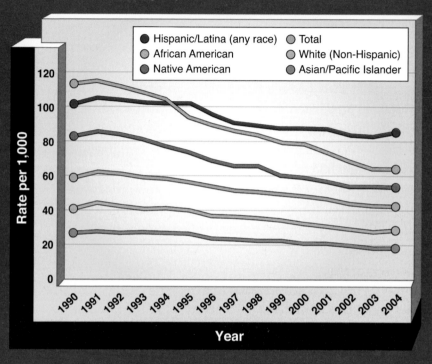

Legend:
- Hispanic/Latina (any race)
- African American
- Native American
- Total
- White (Non-Hispanic)
- Asian/Pacific Islander

Rate per 1,000 vs *Year* (1990–2004)

Taken from: Erika Johanna Vexler and Katherine Suellentrop, "Bridging Two Worlds, How Teen Pregnancy Prevention Programs Can Better Serve Latino Youth," National Campaign to Prevent Pregnancy, January 2006, p. 12. www.thenationalcampaign.org.

teen pregnancy rate among Hispanic girls had gone up. The report also points to teen pregnancy as the leading cause in girls dropping out of high school, and that nearly 1 in 4 Latinas would, in fact, leave school. Try to imagine how such news goes over in a conference room full of professional, college-educated Latinas working on a magazine dedicated to the empowerment of Hispanic women.

The statistics were more disturbing than anyone expected: 51 percent of U.S. Latinas would get pregnant before they turned 20. I remember whispering that awful number to myself, then realizing it meant something unspeakably sad: that a Hispanic teen girl was more likely than not to wind up pregnant. That the exception was now the girl who *didn't* get pregnant.

I've written and edited various stories on those statistics since then. I've read explanations and insights from countless experts, who all point to a lack of educational programs, a desperate need for role models and more parental supervision, and an abundance of casual sex in the media as core causes of teen pregnancy. Most recently, I signed on as chair to the Hispanic Media Advisory Board for The National Campaign to Prevent Teen & Unplanned Pregnancy, a Washington DC–based non-profit, in an effort to encourage Hispanic media outlets everywhere to spread the group's message. What's happened since then? The rate of Hispanic girls getting pregnant grew to 52 percent.

Motherhood. It holds a magical place in all cultures, especially in ours. And family . . . That's what we're all about, isn't it? So when a young girl becomes pregnant, how can a culture that venerates motherhood and family regard it as anything but a blessing? Sometimes it feels as though it's forbidden to look at it any other way.

Yet the harsh reality is that most of the Hispanic girls who become pregnant before they turn 20 will drop out of high school, which will subsequently unleash a series of challenges in their lives and in the lives of their children. As a teen mom, you are almost certain not to graduate from college before the age of 30. One in four teen moms will wind up on welfare. Some 66 percent of the children will live in economically disadvantaged homes and be likelier to suffer from ADD [attention deficit disorder]. Sons of teen moms are likelier to land in juvenile jail, daughters more likely to become teen moms themselves.

"This issue is not a problem exclusive to the Hispanic community," says Marisa Nightingale, senior advisor at The National Campaign to Prevent Teen & Unplanned Pregnancy. "But tackling this issue will also address a host of other social challenges."

A Crisis Facing the Latino Community

I would argue teen pregnancy—not immigration, diabetes, or poverty—is the biggest crisis facing our community, and the nation. In just a few years, Latinos will represent nearly 25 percent of the U.S. population. If more than half our young girls (not to mention all those young dads) become teen parents, it means a significant portion of the American population will not finish high school. Any group's ability to compete economically depends on having an educated workforce. The quality of life of any society depends on having educated, empowered citizens. "What concerns us most," says Nightingale, "is not only what teenage parents will be missing out on today, but the challenges they will face in the future."

Schools Can Find Creative Solutions

It's a Saturday morning and Dr. Mary Jane Garza is calling me from her office at the West Oso School District in Corpus Christi, Texas. An assistant superintendent, she's putting in extra hours on her day off. I've tracked her down because I've been told she runs one of the most successful teen pregnancy programs in the country.

I tell her about the Hispanic teen pregnancy statistics I've been seeing for so long and, of course, she knows them well. She sees them play out in front of her every day. "When I arrived here in 2002, there were 16 pregnant girls at the high school," she says. "They were all dropping out. It was a serious problem."

She and her team instituted some revolutionary tactics. They stopped segregating the pregnant girls and instead had them remain part of the regular student body. The school nurse and an at-risk counselor check in on them at least once a week. The school provides bus transportation and parenting classes. If the pregnant girl has doctor's orders to stay in bed, the school dispatches a teacher to provide lessons at home. After the baby arrives, day care services are arranged.

"You have to think creatively," she says. "Did I get extra funding for this? No. We cover the expenses with what we already get from the state and the federal government. There's always a way to figure it out if you really believe you should."

The turn-around at West Oso is nothing short of remarkable. The pregnancy rate has dramatically decreased—the opposite of what has happened nationally. Garza attributes the decline, in part to the pregnant girls not being segregated. "The other girls see exactly what she's going through," Garza notes, "They see it's not easy. It's a great deterrent." And the pregnant girl? "We've had a 100 percent graduation rate for the last four years."

More than a thousand miles away in Maryland, Maria Gomez is the executive director and founder of Mary's Center, a non-profit facility that provides, health care, social and literacy services to some 16,000 immigrants, many of them undocumented Central Americans. About half the clients are children and teens; too many are already parents themselves.

Because the center treats the teen parents as well as their children, Gomez gets to see the crisis from a unique vantage point. I tell her I've heard babies of teen moms aren't as healthy as others.

Over half of Latina teens have babies before they are twenty, and a quarter of them drop out of high school.

"Actually," she says, "what we have found is that these teens have pretty healthy babies." She pauses, "Physically."

"The problem," she goes on, "is with the child's social development. Because Mom is so unprepared, the child is often cared for by several people." Mom, Dad, Grandma, sisters, friends, anyone who will help. A lot of times there's no schedule for sleeping, eating, playing, because Mom is running around trying to get by. This leads to over-stimulation, which leads to the brain not growing the way it needs to grow. It's hard on Mom and very hard on the babies."

The children who find their way here fall into three categories: those born in the U.S. to undocumented parents; those who crossed the border with their parents as kids; and those who were left behind in their native countries by parents who came to the U.S., only to be abruptly brought over years later. Those, Gomez says, have it the hardest; they feel abandoned, then suddenly find themselves living with a parent who's a virtual stranger. Gomez can hardly hold back her tears when she talks about them. I can't imagine how she copes with seeing these cases every day. And while I realize there are no easy solutions, I ask: What can those of us who are so far from this devastating reality do?

Latina Teens Need Role Models

"What these kids desperately need are role models" she says. "Those of us who've made it, who've had the privilege to get to this country a different way—we too often forget about mentoring. We all received help when we got here from someone. We need to pay that favor back."

I was skeptical at first, but I agree with Gomez. After all the stories I've written and edited, after all the research and programs I've learned about, here's what I've come to believe; that a teen will be less likely to become pregnant if she is absolutely convinced of the possibility of her life. Convinced that she is worthy, that her mind can do as much as her body. That, yes, she can be a mom, but she can do whatever else she wants first. And those of us who already know that because we've lived it—we must do the convincing.

THREE

Being a Teen Father Is Challenging

Wendy Grossman

> Wendy Grossman is a journalist in the Washington, DC, area. This viewpoint follows the life of one teenage father, Christian, as he learns what it means to be a parent. Grossman highlights the changes that have happened in Christian's life from the time he found out his girlfriend was pregnant when he was only fifteen. These changes include having to work to support his daughter, giving up some time that would have been spent with his friends or playing video games, and learning how to take care of a child. Grossman stresses the importance of a teenage father's involvement in his child's life.

The summer is usually a great time for teenagers. School is out, the weather is warm, and you can spend all day with your friends. But in 2006, Christian Moreno's summer was interrupted by some startling news for him: He was going to be a father.

His girlfriend, Darlene Taylor, had been feeling light-headed and experiencing bouts of nausea, two symptoms of pregnancy. A visit to the doctor confirmed that she was going to have a baby. When she called Christian and told him, he thought she was joking. "This can't be happening," he recalls saying at the time.

"I was angry and frustrated that it happened to me," Christian, now 20, tells *Choices*. "I didn't want to be another person with another kid. There were so many young people getting pregnant around me. I didn't want to be like them. I didn't want to have a child. I thought it would ruin my life."

Living Together Is Like Marriage

Christian had dreams of attending college and becoming a social worker. All of that got put on hold. When Darlene was six months pregnant, she moved in with Christian and his parents in their home in Washington, D.C.

Darlene and Christian had met in eighth grade. As a couple, they had spent almost every afternoon hanging out together. But as expectant parents, they fought constantly, even over little things, like where to put clothes: Darlene wanted Christian to hang his clothes in the closet, and he wanted to leave them out. "Every other day, there would be an argument," Christian says.

And when he went out with his friends, Darlene felt abandoned. "She was very clingy and needy," Christian says. "Living with each other is basically marriage—you can't get away. If you go out, and the other person is by herself, she's going to notice if you're not there."

They did have some touching moments. During one doctor's visit, a sonogram, a type of medical imaging, revealed that Darlene was pregnant with a girl. Christian saw the growing baby inside his girlfriend and cried. "I was like, 'Wow, there really is another person in there. She's actually a little person who is mine, who I made,'" he says.

But the pressure of becoming a parent was mounting. Christian had a job as a janitor—a necessity since he and Darlene needed money to care for their child. But as a result, Christian had to leave the hospital when Darlene went into labor. The reason? He was scheduled to clean an office building and couldn't miss work.

"I didn't really want to leave, but I had to go to work," Christian says. Half an hour after he left, Darlene went into the delivery room. She called him that night and told him he was a father.

Teen fathers are confronted with daunting challenges, including working to support the mother and baby, giving up time spent with friends, and learning how to raise a child.

"I just broke down crying," Christian says. "I was so upset that I wasn't there for her. But her friend was there, and she got to cut the cord. They took some pictures, but that really hurt me."

The next morning, he met his daughter: Mikayla Renee Moreno. After the baby was born, Christian and Darlene shared a twin bed. Mikayla slept in her car seat on the floor. There wasn't room for a crib.

Being a Dad Takes Time

Once school started in the fall, they enrolled Mikayla in a government-paid day-care center across the street from the high school. Still, after dropping his daughter off, Christian was often 15 to 20 minutes late for his first-period AP calculus class, "That was really tough," he says. "I was not used to waking up that early. My teacher told me that was no excuse."

For the first several months, Christian mostly let Darlene and his mother care for Mikayla. After school, he worked a six-hour shift cleaning offices to pay for the baby's diapers and formula. When he got home, he was tired and hungry and just wanted to relax and play *Mortal Kombat*. But while he was working, Darlene was watching Mikayla—and by the time he got home, she wanted a break.

"I would try to help out, but I would just end up playing video games," Christian says. On weekdays, his mother watched the baby while he did homework; on weekends, he went out with his friends, which angered Darlene.

One day, Darlene got so exasperated that she told Christian she was going out and promptly left him alone with Mikayla. "I was terrified," he says. Christian had never watched the baby on his own. He didn't know what to feed her, or how to prepare her bottle. "I had no idea how to watch her," he says. "I was always used to somebody helping me out, or somebody doing it for me."

Learning to Be a Dad Is Hard Work

After spending a whole day alone with Mikayla, he realized how much work it was to care for her. "It was tough," Christian says. "You don't have anybody there to take a turn for you if you're tired or want to take a break. I said to Darlene, 'How did you manage? I can't believe you were handling this all by yourself.'"

Christian doesn't remember his dad ever giving him a bath, reading him a story, or tucking him into bed. His mom was the

Births by Father's Age, Over a Five-Year Period

Nearly two-thirds of births that result from an unplanned pregnancy were fathered by men under age thirty.

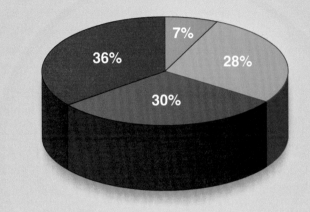

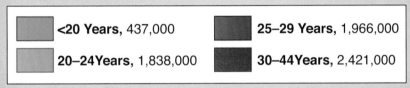

	<20 Years, 437,000		25–29 Years, 1,966,000
	20–24 Years, 1,838,000		30–44 Years, 2,421,000

Taken from: The National Campaign to Prevent Teen and Unplanned Pregnancy, DCR Report (Data, Charts, Research). www.thenationalcampaign.org.

one who took care of him. His dad was either at his job or doing work around the house. "He was there, but that's it," Christian says. "It's been tough trying to build a relationship with him. I don't think he had a father when he grew up, so he never really knew how to be a father."

As a result, Christian says, no one taught [Christian] how to be a good dad. So he's learning with help from Healthy Generations, a program for teen parents and their children at Children's National Medical Center in Washington, D.C.

"People underestimate how important young fathers are," says Dr. Lee Beers, the pediatrician who founded Healthy Generations. Beers has worked with more than 200 teen dads, including Christian.

The program helps young dads work on everything from playing with their kids to creating a résumé. For instance, Christian learned that he should snuggle up with Mikayla when he reads to her and let her follow along with the book. Christian had to learn this because no one read to him when he was a child.

Another positive decision Christian and Darlene made was to stay in school after their daughter was born. Both earned high school diplomas in 2008. Darlene is now studying nursing, and Christian attended community college to become a social worker. Recently, though, he decided to become a minister.

Christian and Darlene are no longer a couple. They broke up after Mikayla's third birthday. Darlene moved to a nearby apartment. But they are still both in their daughter's life. They don't have a set schedule as to who takes care of Mikayla and when. They ask her if she wants to go to Mommy's or Daddy's home after school. As as result, Christian usually sees Mikayla about half the week.

Mikayla is 4 years old now, speaks Spanish to her grandmother, wears her hair in braids, and likes to watch episodes of *Barney*. Her favorite thing to do with Christian is to read books. She also likes it when he helps her get dressed.

Christian has learned that being a parent is a full-time job that can be enervating. "Spending time with kids, you really have to stop what you're doing, and you really have to be there," he says. "You have to make an effort. I could let her watch *Barney* all day, but that wouldn't be spending time with her."

Still, he admits that often he just doesn't feel like spending time with her. He'd rather play video games, listen to music, or just hang out with friends. Sometimes he still spends a whole day in his room, letting his mother watch Mikayla.

He feels bad about that. "I'm trying to work on that," he says. "I'm trying to get to know her."

FOUR

Children of Teen Parents Are Disadvantaged

Denise Rinaldo

> Denise Rinaldo writes articles and books for children. In this viewpoint, she tells the story of Jesseca, who became a mom at sixteen. Jesseca stayed in school after her daughter was born and works to earn money to care for her. Even so, she only has money for the necessities. She is happy to have some things many teen moms do not have—a job, day care, a car—and is able to give her daughter all the love she needs, but she wishes she had waited until she had money and a career so that she could give her daughter more. She encourages other teens to wait until they are older before having children.

Fewer kids are having kids! That was the good news in the United States for 15 years. From 1990 to 2005, the teenage birth rate fell by a whopping 38 percent. But that positive trend seems to have come to an end. In the last two years for which figures are available, the teen birth rate climbed, jumping 3.4 percent in 2006 and 1.4 percent in 2007.

Researchers hope the upward trend will reverse in the coming years. Even with the big drop in teen births over the past decade and a half, the U.S. still has the highest teen birth rate in the industrialized world. It's twice as high as the rates in England and Canada.

It's eight times higher than the rates in the Netherlands and Japan. Three out of 10 teenage girls in the U.S. get pregnant at least once before age 20, which amounts to 745,000 teen pregnancies each year.

Teens who become mothers are more likely to experience poverty than those who wait until they're older to have children. Teen

Diploma/GED Attainment by Age Twenty-Two

Teen mothers have lower high school diploma attainment than those who did not have a teen birth.

Teen Birth (age 19 or younger)

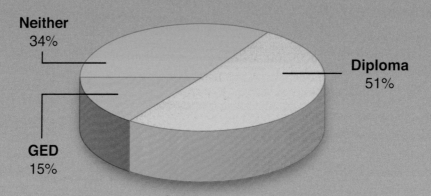

Neither
34%

Diploma
51%

GED
15%

No Teen birth

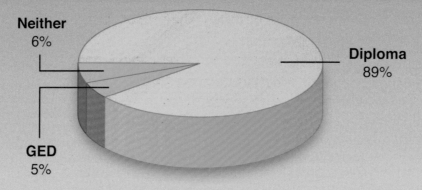

Neither
6%

Diploma
89%

GED
5%

Taken from: Kate Perper, et al., "Diploma Attainment Among Teen Mothers," *Child Trends Fact Sheet*, January 2010. www.childtrends.org.

moms are also much more likely than other teens to drop out of school. The babies of teen mothers are more likely to have low birth weights, which puts them at risk for illness and even death.

Starting below is the story of one teen mom. She is working hard to do her best for herself and her daughter. But, drawing on her experience, she has this advice for teens: Wait until you're older to have children.

A Downward Spiral

Jesseca Heatherly was 16 years old, and she'd had a tough two years. Her father died when she was 14. Her grief sent her into a downward spiral. She started abusing drugs, and in her junior year of high school, she dropped out.

"Then, I started feeling really sick," Jesseca tells *Choices*. "I was cold, I was throwing up all the time, I didn't know what was wrong."

A health-clinic employee delivered the stunning news: Jesseca was pregnant. "It was really scary," Jesseca says. "I didn't know what to do. I couldn't believe it." She told her boyfriend. "He was in shock," Jesseca says. Though the pregnancy came as a surprise to Jesseca and her boyfriend. It shouldn't have. They had been having sex regularly but never used birth control.

"I ought to have been thinking about birth control, but I just wasn't," Jesseca says. She mistakenly believed that the drugs she was abusing were so bad for her body that she wouldn't be able to get pregnant. That was a myth. In fact, research shows that teens who abuse drugs or alcohol are more likely to become pregnant because substance abuse clouds a person's judgment.

Teen Moms Have to Grow Up Fast

Until she found out she was pregnant, Jesseca had imagined a certain future for herself. She had planned to return to school and resume an ordinary teenage life. "I'd always been involved in sports," she says. "I loved spending the night at friends' houses. I wanted to do all that again. I wanted to go to the prom."

Jesseca assumed she'd have the freedom to go to college and choose a career. "I would always say I wasn't going to get married or pregnant until I was 30 years old," she says.

She quickly learned that her life as a teen mom would be very different from what she'd imagined for herself. "I had to grow up really quickly," Jesseca says. She swore off drugs and alcohol. Through a friend, she heard about a program for adolescent parents run by an organization called the Children and Family Resource Center. It was close by, in her hometown of Hendersonville, North Carolina. The group helped her get medical care while she was pregnant and helped her enroll in an alternative high school with an on-site day-care center.

When she was 17, Jesseca gave birth to a baby girl. She named her Izabella, but calls her Bella for short. "The first time I held her, I was so scared," Jesseca says. "I was afraid I wasn't going to do it right."

Six weeks later, Jesseca returned to school, baby in tow. "There were times when Bella would be up crying all night long," Jesseca says. "It was so difficult having to wake up the next morning and get her ready, then get myself ready. I thought of quitting [school] all the time."

Most Teen Moms Quit School

But she didn't. Jesseca graduated from high school last year. This was a huge accomplishment. Faced with the pressures of parenting, most teen moms give up on their education. Parenthood is the leading reason that teen girls quit school. Fewer than half of teen mothers graduate from high school, and fewer than 2 percent earn a college degree by the time they turn 30 years old.

With the help of Summer Stipe, coordinator of the adolescent parenting program that Jesseca joined, the teen got a job at a day-care center and applied to college. Last fall, Jesseca enrolled in Blue Ridge Community College. She is majoring in early childhood education.

Bella is now 16 months old. Between school, work, and caring for Bella, Jesseca has absolutely no free time. "Literally, every single hour of Jesseca's day is scheduled," Stipe says. "She works during the day and goes to classes at night."

Raising a Child Is Expensive

Despite receiving financial aid for school and a government grant for day care, money is also extremely tight. I don't have nice clothes," Jesseca says. "I don't buy makeup. I just have necessities. I don't buy things for myself; I buy them for my daughter."

Teen parents typically start child rearing with several disadvantages: Many have no job, do not own a car—much less have money for day care—and may have quit school due to their parenting responsibilities.

But it isn't the financial struggle or the lack of free time that is Jesseca's biggest concern. It is her longing to give Bella what she herself never had; a happy childhood with loving parents. "More than anything, she wants Bella to grow up with a mom and dad who love each other," Stipe says.

As a teen mom, Jesseca has the deck stacked against her. When their babies are born, more than half of unmarried teen mothers say either that they are "sure" or "chances are good" that they will marry the father of their child, according to a survey by the National Campaign to Prevent Teen and Unwanted Pregnancy. Eighty percent of the time, however, that never happens.

Whether it will happen for Jesseca remains to be seen. She is still involved with Bella's father, and they have lived together off and on. She works hard at the relationship because it is so important to her, but it is rocky. "I'll leave him, than I'll come back," Jesseca says. "It's kind of a messy situation."

Still, Jesseca is more fortunate than many teen mothers. Her baby's father contributes financially, she has a job and day care for her child, and she is moving forward with her education. Her uncle gave her a car, which enables her to go to work and college. As is the case in most of the U.S., public transportation is scarce in Henderson County, where Jesseca lives. Without a car a person is stuck at home, which is sadly the case for most teen moms. "Out of 40 girls in the adolescent parenting program, only four have cars," Stipe says.

Jesseca can't imagine life without Bella. I couldn't love her any more than I do," she says. But Jesseca knows that her life and Bella's would have been easier if she had waited to get pregnant. Her advice to teens: "Wait until you're older. If I'd waited, I could have had money and a career that I really wanted. Now, I have to rely on other people to get what I need. If you have a child when you're a teen, you're never going to be able to give your child everything you want to give him or her."

FIVE

Babies of Teen Fathers Are Born with Greater Health Challenges

Jane Bainbridge

Jane Bainbridge is a journalist who lives in the United Kingdom. In this viewpoint, she discusses a 2007 study that reported on the influence of the father's age on the condition of babies at birth. The study showed that babies born to fathers under the age of twenty were more likely to be born early, have low birth weight, and have a low score on the Apgar test, which is given within five minutes of birth and measures skin tone, pulse rate, reaction to stimulation, muscle tone, and breathing. Although the study did not determine what causes these problems, the author concludes that one cause could be the inability of teenage fathers to provide sufficient emotional and financial support to their partners.

Unsurprisingly the great focus of childbirth and childrearing is on the mother. Is she: eating the right things; taking enough exercise; too old/too young; breastfeeding or weaning her baby at the right age? Does she provide her children with their five-a-day [servings of fruit and vegetables], intellectually stimulate them, play age-appropriate games, and so forth? When measuring up the opportunities for a child it is invariably against a yardstick of criteria for the mother.

With so much attention placed on the mother's capabilities it is sometimes as if the father's role is minimal. Once his sperm has worked its magic, his genetic imprint cast, he is then a benign bystander in his children's upbringing.

If the father gets a nod of acknowledgement it is usually only in a negative context. The absentee father may be criticised for the rise in delinquency or gang culture but even then the media quickly shifts the focus and blame back on the mothers raising their children single-handedly.

So if the role of the father is lucky enough to be accredited it will often be for older children, when the father's influence is most apparent.

A study has shown that many babies born to fathers under the age of twenty are more likely to be born prematurely, have a low birth weight, and score poorly on the Apgar test, which assesses the health of newborns.

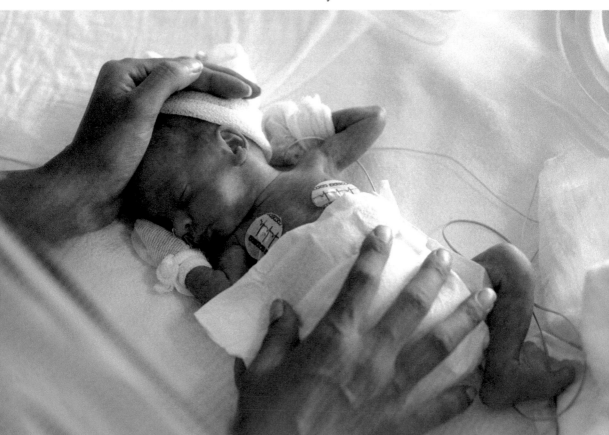

The Father's Influence at Birth

But what of at birth; what is the father's influence with unborn babies and childbirth? A supportive and caring father is clearly hugely beneficial to both the mother and baby during this period and mothers with partners actively involved at this stage are at a significant advantage.

But a study recently published in *Human Reproduction* journal (2007) casts a whole new light on the role and influence of fathers. Research carried out at the Ottawa Health Research Institute in Canada found that teenage fathers are at increased risk of having babies born with birth problems. These problems can range from pre-term delivery, low birth weight to death during or near delivery.

So used are we to seeing these kind of studies carried out with a maternal focus that it almost demands a double-take of the reader to see that the research is looking at the risk associated with the age of the father at birth.

For women the headlines and studies on their age are typically about how less likely older mothers are to conceive or the increased complications in childbirth related to maternal age. But in this study the correlation found was that it was younger fathers that had associated problems while older fathers, aged 40 or more, were not at increased risk of having babies affected by these problems.

This is no small scale research project either. Indeed the study is the largest yet carried out on the effects of paternal age on adverse birth outcomes and the results were independent of the age or other factors of the mother that might have an impact on birth.

It looked at US data on the births that took place between 1995 and 2000, which equated to almost 24 million births. The data was honed to look just at single live births and all the mothers were married, it was their first baby and they were aged between 20- and 29-years-old. They also needed to have complete information on the father, including age and race as well as good details on the babies' pre-natal care, birth weight, etc. This brought the number down to just over 2.5 million.

The maternal age range was fixed as these women are least likely to have fertility problems, which can have an impact on birth

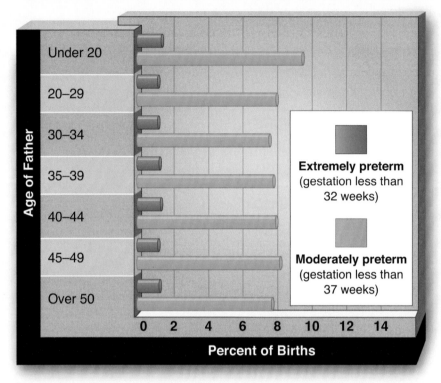

Taken from: Xi-Kuan Chen, et al., "Paternal Age and Adverse Birth Outcomes: Teenager or 40+, Who Is at Risk?" *Human Reproduction*, February 7, 2008, p. 1293.

outcomes. Because fathers in the same age range have the lowest risk of adverse birth outcomes it was used as the reference group for all other ages to be compared against.

Babies of Teen Fathers Have Health Problems

What the researchers found was that babies born to fathers under the age of 20 were more likely to be born early, have low birth weight, be small for gestational age and have a low Apgar score. [Apgar score measures the newborn baby's skin color, pulse rate, reaction to stimulation, muscle tone, and breathing]. There was also a raised risk of the babies dying in the first four weeks after birth (22% increased risk). This rose to a 41% increased risk of the baby dying between four weeks and one year after birth. There was no increased risk for older fathers. The results clearly show being a teenage father was an independent risk factor for adverse birth outcomes and that further investigation was needed.

Causes Are Unclear

What is not clear from this study is whether the adverse outcomes are a result of biological or socio-economic factors. There was no information available on the lifestyles of the fathers to determine the influence of social factors.

Previous studies have pointed to biological factors with younger men sometimes having lower sperm counts, semen volume and percentage of mobile sperm. Immature sperm may result in problems in the formation of the placenta which can affect the outcome of the birth.

But clearly there could equally be socio-economic factors at play. More young fathers might come from disadvantaged families and be less educated. In all walks of the health service socio-economic factors such as education and occupation are known to affect health outcomes. This demographic is less likely to use pre-natal services. Teenage fathers might also be more likely to smoke, drink alcohol and take illegal drugs.

More research in this area would be welcome, but I can't help feeling that the fact that it is simply harder for teenagers to provide the emotional and financial support that their partners need at this time has a lot to do with it.

SIX

Telling the Family Is a Challenge for Teen Parents

Joanna Gregson

Joanna Gregson is an associate professor of sociology at Pacific Lutheran University in Tacoma, Washington. She spent four years studying moms at the Teen Center, a teenage parenting program at a local high school, for her book *The Culture of Teenage Mothers*. In this viewpoint, excerpted from that book, Gregson states that telling the family about the pregnancy is one of the most difficult parts of being an expectant teen parent. She uses the stories of expectant teen mothers to illustrate the reactions that families have when told about a pregnancy. Most family members are shocked at first but eventually become accepting. Some are accepting from the moment they find out, and some are angry and remain that way.

Most of the teen mothers [that I interviewed] told me the thing they feared most about their pregnancy was the fact that they would have to tell their parents. Regardless of whether they were happy about the pregnancy or upset about it, they were practically unanimous in their fear of telling their parents. [Naomi] Farber noted a similar pattern in her study of adolescent mothers, commenting, "Fear was a common reaction both before and especially after confirmation of their pregnancy, often because of the antici-pated response of their parents to the news". Many of the young women at the Teen Center [a teen parenting program located at a high school], like the women in [Gillian] Schofield's study of teen mothers, were so scared about the prospect of telling their parents that they put off telling them for several months. Given the tremendous influence parents, especially mothers, have on ado-lescents' decisions regarding pregnancy resolution, the reactions of their parents were crucial in shaping their choices to carry their pregnancies to term and to raise their babies themselves.

Initial Shock, Eventual Acceptance

[Sharon] Thompson explained that the general sequence of events among the teens in her study who told their parents they were pregnant was "family drama," followed by shock, back-and-forth debates about how she should resolve the issue, and, ultimately, some degree of tolerance, acceptance, or support. Farber recount-ed similar stories of the young mothers in her study and noted that although most white and black pregnant teens anticipated anger as their parents' first reaction, the white teens were more likely to be met with parental concern, unhappiness, or disap-pointment than anger. These sentiments resemble descriptions given by white Teen Center participants as well. For example, nineteen-year-old Julie told me that her mother and sister were both shocked when she became pregnant the first time at age sixteen, despite the fact that her older sister had two children as a teenager. By the time she became pregnant for the third time, they were less than pleased:

> I mean, with this one, my mom, instead of saying "Congratulations!" she said "Well I'm sorry to hear you're pregnant again." My mom only had two kids and she's had abortions every time after that. And my sister, well, she didn't say, "I'm sorry." She asked what I was going to do and I told her I was going to keep him. And she was like, "Oh, OK. As long as you know what you want to do." But I could tell that she thought I was making a mistake.

"A grandmother at my age!" cartoon by Mike Lynch.www.CartoonStock.com.

By the time Julie was in her second trimester, however, both her mother and sister had come around; her mother gave Julie a car so she and her sons could get to school easier when the baby arrived, and her sister volunteered to babysit the three boys if Julie ever wanted to leave them at home.

Seventeen-year-old Andrea, who became pregnant after dating her boyfriend for three weeks, had to face telling her grandmother, who had raised her since she was three years old. After Andrea's younger sister's pregnancy, her grandmother put tremendous pressure on Andrea to finish high school and to go to college before starting a family, and she was disappointed when Andrea also became pregnant. Andrea told me her grandmother initially asked her to move out of the house, but added that her anger did not last long: when Andrea had complications early in her second trimester, it was her grandmother who took her to the hospital and cared for her when she returned home.

Fifteen-year-old Vanessa was so afraid of telling her parents about her pregnancy that she kept it a secret from them until she was five months along:

> I was scared to tell my mom. Really scared. And when I did finally tell her, she got really upset. She went through her denial thing, you know, saying it couldn't be true 'cause I was too young and everything. But after a while she started to accept it, and now she loves the baby. My stepdad was furious. He made my mom send me to live with my dad in Texas during my pregnancy because he didn't want me around embarrassing him or whatever. And my dad, oh, he was so mad! But he came around after I was out there with him, and I guess my stepdad is okay with it now that I'm living with them again, but I don't really ever talk to him because I hate him so much.

Like Andrea's grandmother and Julie's mother and sister, Vanessa's parents were disappointed in her and let her know it, but the disappointment gave way to acceptance once the baby was born.

Many of the teens told me they received different reactions from their mothers and fathers. [Researchers Michael] Bracken, [Lorraine] Klerman, and [Maryann] Bracken posited that pregnant teens often turn first to people they think will be supportive and avoid "authority figures" they think will be angry with them or disagree with their decisions for resolution. At the Teen Center, the supportive person was usually the adolescent's mother, and the authority figure was her father. The teens were unanimous in telling me that their mothers were more supportive about the pregnancy than their fathers and, perhaps anticipating this support, they usually told their mothers first. . . .

Only one teen with whom I spoke thought her parents would be supportive of her pregnancy, and it turned out she was wrong.

Fourteen-year-old Angelica, who intentionally became pregnant, said she figured her parents had no choice but to be supportive:

> I mean, they couldn't really be mad because I was already married. My mom, she didn't talk to me, or she ignored me, for about a week. But we're best friends now. My dad was mean though. 'Cause the stupid thing he did is told my mom, "It's either Angelica and the baby or me." 'Cause he thought him and my mom should disown me for getting pregnant. And my mom said, "Well, I guess you gotta leave." Because, see, my friend had just had a baby—she's the one who introduced me to my husband—and my dad was like, "Oh, are you going to go and copy her?" I'm like, "You don't go copy someone to go get pregnant." But that's what he thought I did. And he gave my mom this, "Either choose me or choose her," and my mom said, "My kids always come first." So he didn't like that very much, and he left.

Whereas Angelica's decision to marry at an early age was enthusiastically supported by her Latino mother and father who, she told me later, expected all of their daughters to marry before they were twenty, her parents did not subscribe to the cultural norm for young married women to begin child rearing as soon as possible. This stance may have been a result of their location in a well-educated, affluent, university community. In Lakeside, [Washington,] education was clearly the path to success, and Angelica's parents may have seen having a child as interfering with her chance for achieving the success they wanted for her.

Immediate Acceptance

In Schofield's study of teen mothers, several of the adolescents' mothers were described as being excited about the pregnancy from the moment they learned of it. Although this was not as common at the Teen Center, a few young women recounted similar stories. For example, seventeen-year-old Sunshine told me her mother was thrilled when she learned the news: "My mom, she was like

Most teen mothers have said that the thing they feared most about being pregnant was informing their parents of the pregnancy and being fearful of their reactions.

totally excited because she was going to have her first grandbaby." Sunshine had not seen nor heard from her mother from the time she was three years old until she was thirteen because her father's parents raised her and her brother after her parents divorced. Sunshine explained to me that she and her mom "weren't like mother-daughter," but more like friends because of the long time they had been apart, and she thought that might have explained why her mother took the news better than the mothers of some of her Teen Center friends. . . .

A significant number of the teens told me they did not expect their families to be as supportive of their pregnancies as they were. Twenty-year-old Brooke was afraid to tell her parents that she and her boyfriend were expecting a baby. In fact, she hid in the bathroom with the door locked while her boyfriend broke the news to her parents. She told me she was pleasantly surprised when "they were supportive from day one." Perhaps because they belonged to the Church of Jesus Christ of Latter-day Saints, the idea of Brooke beginning her family at a young age was not as terrible as she thought it might be, especially since she and her boyfriend were engaged. Similarly, seventeen-year-old Jessica told me her mother was thrilled about the baby, and she too thought it might have been her mother's religious background that softened the blow:

I told my mom right away when I thought I was pregnant. She's the one who made the appointment actually. She was really excited about it, really excited because she thought it was a sign from God. Especially when she found out it was a boy because you see I have four sisters and you know, some religious people think they need to have a son for some reason. My mother is different. She's really religious—she's a religious zealot. She started kind of getting under the impression that this was a child that was going to be sent to her through me from God.

Jessica was one of the few teens who told her mother she might be pregnant before she knew for sure herself. Most of the other teens told me they took pregnancy tests first, then told their mothers. . . .

Prolonged Anger

A small number of teens told me the initial shock and anger expressed by their parents never wore off, that their relationships had been irreparably damaged by their pregnancies. In every case, the fathers were the ones who showed continual disappointment in their daughters, or expressed unwavering anger toward the men who had done this to their daughters. Mothers may have expressed these feelings initially, but by the time the baby was born, they had forgiven their daughters.

LaNiece's story is a good example of this difference in how family members reacted to the pregnancy. Her mother was excited about the prospect of becoming a grandmother from the moment she found out about her daughter's pregnancy, her two brothers were disappointed but supportive, and her father was angry:

My dad was mad. He was always shooting at him, at my son's dad. You know, he'd take out his gun and whenever Shawn would come by he'd *shoot* at him to scare him off! And my brothers, oh my gosh, my brothers were so mad and they beat him up so bad. Shawn was like two or three years older than my big brother, and a lot of times my brother used to be scared of him because he was older, but my god, he just beat him up. But they weren't mad at me, which was weird. My brothers were supportive. They would always try to touch my stomach or feel him kicking. They, I don't know, they felt kind of bad; my older brother would say, "Oh you messed up your life, you'll never do anything." But my dad, he didn't want to talk about it then, and now it's almost three years later, and he still barely talks to me.

Seventeen-year-old Sunshine's father did not go as far as shooting at his grandson's father, but he let Sunshine know he was disappointed with her through the first comment he made to her after she told him she was having a baby. Because she was so afraid of his reaction, she waited until the month before the baby was born to call and tell him she was pregnant: "When I first told my dad, I was like eight months' pregnant. And his reaction was—he wasn't shocked. He said he was wondering when it was going to happen, which kind of pissed me off but I didn't let him know that." She went on to tell me that this was his way of saying that nothing she could do would surprise him, because she had already disappointed him so much.

SEVEN

Teen Fathers Face Social Stigmas

Mark S. Kiselica

Mark S. Kiselica is a psychologist and counselor who has spent a good deal of his career working with teenage fathers. In this viewpoint, taken from his book *When Boys Become Parents*, Kiselica discusses some of the problems regarding how society treats teenage fathers and some of the difficulties teenage fathers face. He says that the negative stereotypes of teenage fathers as callous and uncaring are often untrue. He notes that counseling and social services for young parents are often focused on girls only. Boys need help in learning to be fathers, and Kiselica encourages adults to make an effort to understand these boys and to provide services for them.

Foremost, my work with teen fathers has taught me to move beyond societal stereotypes about boys who become fathers during their teenage years. These stereotypes are widespread and they have destructive effects. For example, a common belief about adolescent fathers is that they are a callous lot who purposely exploit, seduce, and impregnate an adolescent girl and then coldly abandon her and her baby. . . . These attitudes permeate our society and explain why too many adults have little sympathy for boys who "get their girlfriends pregnant." These troubling biases persist in spite of considerable evidence suggesting that teen dads deserve much more credit than they typically receive. For example, although it is true that some young fathers have engaged in exploitive and antisocial behavior toward their partners while neglecting their children, the research literature indicates that the majority of teen fathers have a long-term, caring relationship with the adolescent mother prior to and throughout the pregnancy, and that most provide varied forms of emotional and financial support to the mother and baby during the first year of the child's life. After the first year, however, the relationship between the young mother and father tends to deteriorate, and the frequency of contact between the father and his partner and child tends to decline over time.

Pregnancy Presents Dilemmas

A tragic sequence and interaction of problems often cause the faltering relationship between adolescent fathers and their partners and children. To begin with, the couple must confront the emotionally draining dilemma about how to resolve the pregnancy. Should they consider abortion? Adoption? Keep the baby and marry? Keep the baby, forego marriage, but live together? Keep the baby, forego marriage, and live in separate households? These weighty decisions can drive the couple apart, especially if they disagree about which option to pursue.

If the mother decides to keep the baby, then the couple and their families must address the financial responsibilities associated with raising a child, a matter that is complicated by the dire socioeconomic conditions of many teen parents. Adolescent fathers are over represented among the poor and tend to live in neighborhoods characterized by inadequate school systems and high rates of unemployment. Adolescent fathers also tend to drop out of school, either before or after the pregnancy. Thus, they have limited financial resources and employment opportunities, circumstances that make it difficult for them to support a family financially, even though most do try to provide some form of financial support for the child. These financial hardships can strain the relationship between the adolescent parents and their respective families as they all try to cope with the crisis that is precipitated by an unplanned pregnancy.

Additional problems are embedded in the tenuousness of adolescent romantic relationships. The amorous feelings between the

The negative stereotype of teenage fathers as being callous and uncaring in regard to their babies and partners is largely untrue.

young parents often wane and the couple discovers that they are incompatible and have irreconcilable differences. Fights between the teen parents can erupt and feuds between the families of the young parents may break out. In the face of such tensions, the adolescent father, who typically does not have custody of the baby, may be denied access to his child, and he may give up on seeking such access, either because he is unaware of his legal rights to visitation or because he can no longer tolerate the conflicts. The couple drifts apart and the father gradually loses substantive contact with his child. . . .

Teen Fathers Have Many Stresses

So, in the words of Bryan Robinson, a social scientist, former professor at the University of North Carolina at Charlotte, and one of the earliest champions of adolescent fathers, the experience of parenthood for most teen fathers is one of "hard truths and tragic consequences." Indeed, in a series of pioneering studies conducted in the 1980s, Leo Hendricks and his colleagues from Howard University documented that teen fathers experience a variety of stresses associated with their early entry to parenthood, including relationship difficulties with the adolescent mother and her family, lost opportunities to bond with his child, financial hardships, and educational and career concerns. Negotiating these difficulties while mastering the combined developmental challenges of adolescence and parenthood complicates the transition to adulthood. Hendricks suggested that young fathers could be assisted with these challenges by providing counseling and social services tailored to the needs of young fathers. Furthermore, his findings indicated that most adolescent fathers want assistance with their many concerns.

In spite of the expressed concerns of teenage fathers and their desire to receive help, it appears that the needs of this population go largely unnoticed. The results of numerous studies, including several conducted by me and my students and colleagues at Ball State University and The College of New Jersey, have indicated that teenage parenting programs tend

Percent of Births That Result from an Unplanned Pregnancy by Father's Age, 2002

More than half (52 percent) of births to teen boys were the result of an unplanned pregnancy.

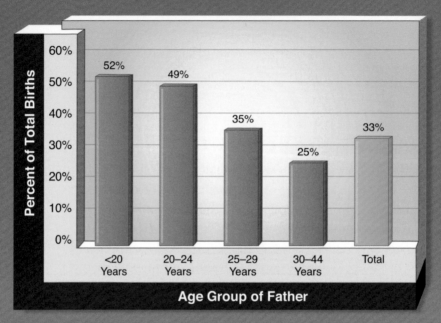

Taken from: The National Campaign to Prevent Teen and Unplanned Pregnancy, DCR Report (Data, Charts, Research). www.thenationalcampaign.org.

to consist of services for adolescent mothers but not for adolescent fathers. Several authorities on the subject of teen fathers have argued that this neglect represents a manifestation of the societal stereotypes about adolescent fathers, which I described earlier. This claim is supported by the findings of studies indicating that many service providers ignore the needs of teen fathers due to their pejorative and inaccurate generalizations about this population.

In light of this inexcusable state of affairs, we are challenged to move beyond stereotypic images of adolescent fathers and to think more complexly about these young men. Achieving this task is a critical first step toward helping teenage boys facing unplanned paternity. It must be followed by persistent efforts to engage adolescent fathers in services designed to assist them with their concerns and their transition to parenthood. . . .

Society Needs to Help Teens Learn to Be Fathers

We cannot expect teen fathers to master the challenges of parenthood if society continues to give these young men the mixed message, "We demand that you become a responsible parent but we won't provide you with the compassionate guidance about how to become one." The continuation of this destructive message will only further alienate adolescent fathers from adults who might be able to assist them to become loving, capable parents. So it's time to change the way we think about and treat teen fathers. We must replace simplistic stereotypes about teen fathers with a more complex understanding of these young men. We must offer teenage boys facing early paternity our compassionate understanding and assistance. We must transform our traditional ways of relating to young fathers into a more male-friendly approach to helping them. At the same time, in an empathic and loving way, we must continue to challenge adolescent fathers who demonstrate harmful conceptions of what it means to be a man and help them to develop alternative, healthier notions of masculinity and to become productive citizens. At all times we must look for, and build upon, the good that exists in all teen fathers. Lastly, if we really intend to help young fathers to develop positive relationships with their children and the mothers of their children, then we all must model tenderness and vulnerability to teen fathers by speaking to them from our hearts.

EIGHT

Teen Parents Are Helping in School Programs to Discourage Teen Pregnancy

Sharon Jayson

> Sharon Jayson is a behavior and relationships reporter for *USA Today*. In this viewpoint, she discusses new programs that started in Texas and are spreading to other states as an alternative to sex education. In these programs, teens who are parents visit high schools and talk about some of the real issues that teen parents face. Students also participate in learning exercises that spark discussion about what it is like to be a teen parent. State officials hope these programs will reduce the number of teens who become parents.

There are no crying-baby dolls here. And no abstinence message, either. Instead, there's plenty of straight talk about relationships, marriage, children and money, all designed to give teenagers—especially boys—a dose of reality about teen parenthood.

"I had to get over myself," Robert Aleman, 19, told teens at Akins High School [in Austin, Texas,] recently. His son, Jonathan, turned 3 last month. "I realized I had to get over what I wanted. . . . My son comes first."

Students are responding.

Sharon Jayson, "Teen Parenting Programs Get Real," *USA Today*, December 15, 2010, p. 1D. Copyright © 2010. Reprinted with permission.

"To me, it was real-life stuff, and scary," says freshman Asa Taylor, 15, who heard Aleman in a class.

It's not necessarily a scare tactic, but in classrooms across Texas, and in a growing number of other states, schools are looking at two new programs that teach teens about the consequences of irresponsible sexual behavior—without either the controversial sex-education quotient or abstinence-focused programs, whose message, educators say, often falls on deaf ears.

The programs, developed by Texas child-support officials, focus on the legal responsibilities, emotional toll and dollars-and-cents realities of life as a teen parent.

An Important New Trend

The approach represents an important new trend in an area that has been controversial and fraught with problems. And because these programs have shown such early promise, they are spreading across the country, as educators and state officials see in them a new way to target high teen birth rates in the USA.

One program is called Parenting and Paternity Awareness (PAPA), and the other is No Kidding, a partnership between community groups that work with school districts.

"People tell us all the time, 'Don't have sex' and 'Use protection,' but it's pretty obvious it doesn't really help, because the rates are still high," says freshman Adriana Garza, 14, who participated in PAPA as part of [teacher] Mandy Thomas' health class at Akins.

The teen birth rate in the USA—41.5 births per 1,000 for girls ages 15–19, according to the most recent federal data for 2008—is much higher than in many other developed countries. For example, the teen birth rate in Switzerland is 4.3 births per 1,000; in Germany, it's 9.9 per 1,000; and in Spain, it's 13.2 per 1,000, according to the United Nations Statistics Division Demographic Yearbook 2007.

Texas Tries New Programs

PAPA is a 14-hour curriculum required for all Texas high school students beginning in fall 2008. More than half a million Texas students took it during the past two school years.

In fall 2009, health classes were no longer mandatory in Texas, but if students take health, they have PAPA, says Cynthia Osborne, an associate professor of public policy at the LBJ [Lyndon Baines Johnson] School of Public Affairs at the University of Texas [UT] in Austin, who directed a team evaluating the program for the attorney general's office. "This is not a sex-education curriculum," she says. "This provides the why you don't want to get pregnant, but not the how."

Osborne's evaluation notes that PAPA is "the first large-scale effort in any state to educate students on parental responsibilities using child support and paternity as the basis for the program."

"PAPA is addressing an unmet need for students, and it is significantly improving students' knowledge and attitudes in areas that are unique to the PAPA curriculum," the evaluation says.

The No Kidding program includes three 50-minute sessions with personal stories from teen parents, as well as information about the legal and financial obligations related to paternity; presenters are paid $40 an hour as peer educators. There is even a Price Is Right–type exercise on the cost of baby items.

"I got that paycheck, and man, that money was gone," says Aleman, who works two jobs and is a part-time community-college student. "The list got longer. There was diapers, there's formula, there's onesies. There's socks. There's wipes. There's the baby seat. There's the car seat. I'm working all this time just so I can be broke."

Aleman shares joint custody with his son's mother, whom he knew casually when she became pregnant. Every Sunday, Jonathan moves between their homes.

According to 2008 data released last week by the National Center for Health Statistics, Texas has the third-highest teen birth rate in the nation, with 63.4 per thousand, behind Mississippi (65.7) and New Mexico (64.1).

An analysis of all births to mothers under 20 in 2008, conducted for USA Today by the non-profit Child Trends, found 19% were repeat teen births. The states with the highest rates of repeat teen births were Mississippi (23%), Texas (22%) and Arizona (22%).

Janece Rolfe of the child-support division in the Texas Office of the Attorney General says her agency developed the educa-

In Texas, as well as in a growing number of other states, schools are looking at new programs that teach teens about the consequences of irresponsible sexual behavior, about their legal and financial responsibilities, and about the emotional toll exacted.

tion programs to "have a more family-centered approach to the child-support process," with the aim of preventing teen parents from ending up on the rolls of child-support enforcement cases. Rolfe says most non-custodial parents are fathers, which is why the programs focus on dads and paternity. As of the end of November [2010], the caseload totaled 1.2 million.

Learning Exercises Spark Conversation

"Fathers are needed for more than a paycheck. It's not just about the financial contribution," Rolfe says. "Our PAPA approach aims to increase father involvement and the concept of co-parenting."

The 14 units include a variety of exercises, games and quizzes that can be taught in various ways over a semester, from 14 school days to once a week for 14 weeks. In Thomas' class, she distributed signs saying "myth" and "truth" to get her students thinking. A "Where Do You Stand?" exercise had students move around the room, discussing whether they agreed or disagreed with statements about marriage and gender. In a marriage circle game, they talked about issues such as love at first sight and the best age to marry.

"I think you should get married at 30," freshman Hugo Jimenez, 14, told his classmates. "You'll finish all your studies and you won't have to worry about marriage and babies and all that stuff, and you'll also have a good career by then, and you'll still have time to party and stuff."

The other peer presenter in Gabriel Mata's freshman class in teen leadership was Sharlene Casaclang, 21, who told students of getting pregnant at 18 as a University of Texas freshman. She had her son, Maynard, 2, when she was 19. She married her son's father, Brandon, now 25, before Maynard was born.

"I never thought about adoption," says Casaclang, now a full-time UT student who returned to college after a year at home with her son. "But I had my selfish stage where I just wanted to up and leave."

These programs do spark talk, say the students.

"I had discussions with my friends about 'What would happen if you were to become a father?'" says senior Taylor Rutland, 17, in

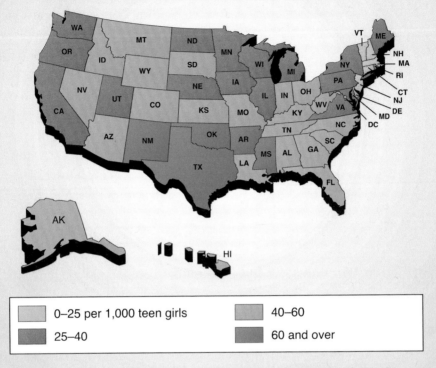

Teen Birth Rates by State, 2008

0–25 per 1,000 teen girls

25–40

40–60

60 and over

Taken from: www.msnbc.msn.com/id/39727979. Based on data from National Center for Health Statistics.

Thomas' health class. "I don't think there's any amount of information that can prepare a teenager . . . for being a parent."

Osborne's evaluation (based on tests of 5,730 students from 47 Texas high schools before and after taking PAPA classes and on focus groups with 75 students) says that after the program, "students' knowledge increases significantly" and "students are less likely to report that they want to have a child prior to marriage."

Data collection is now under way for Osborne's evaluation of the No Kidding program; results will be available this summer [2011]. Currently, No Kidding is available in just three Texas communities—Austin, El Paso and Houston. It's offered district-wide in Austin and the El Paso area and is offered in selected schools in Houston. During the 2009–10 school year, almost 8,800 students participated in the program at school or in community venues, such as after-school programs or the Y [YMCA or YWCA].

Word about PAPA and No Kidding is spreading; versions of the programs are now also being offered at schools in New York City, Los Angeles County and parts of Arkansas, Georgia and Ohio.

"It's very practical knowledge and education about the potential perils and pitfalls of teen pregnancy, from people who have lived it and are living it," says Ben Johnson of Ohio's Department of Job and Family Services, which is offering No Kidding as a pilot program in two counties and plans to expand it statewide.

Aleman says he has learned a lot from being a teen father: "Now that I have a baby, I realize how grown up I wasn't," he says.

In his presentation, he urges high school students not to grow up too fast. "Don't—because once you do, there's no going back. Trust me."

Aleman loves his son and says being a dad helped get him off the street. But, he says, he has regrets.

"I brought him into a world where he doesn't have his parents together. I brought him into a world where he's having to switch homes every other week," he says. "I wasn't ready to be a father. I'm still trying to get my life together and find my place in this world and I'm trying to raise him. I wish I had been ready for him."

NINE

Schools Should Provide Educational Services to Teen Parents and Their Children

Marilyn F. Scholl

Marilyn F. Scholl is supervisor of a teenage parenting program in the Arlington, Virginia, public school system. In this viewpoint, Scholl talks about the need for teen parents to remain in school and the responsibility of schools to provide educational services so that these teens can become self-supporting, economically productive citizens. Having an education will help to prevent unemployment, welfare dependency, and juvenile crime, she contends. She also believes that it is important for the schools to educate not only the teen parents but also their children, who may be at an educational disadvantage because their parents have not yet completed their own education.

Teenage pregnancy is still occurring. What should educators do about adolescent pregnancy? Whose responsibility is it to educate adolescent parents? This article examines the perennial youth challenge of adolescent pregnancy and proactive approaches to curbing the problem through educating young parents.

Adolescent pregnancy remains a persistent problem in the United States. In spite of federal, state, and community attention to this issue, America has faced and continues to face crisis levels of adolescent pregnancy, the highest of any nation in the western world. Annually, more than 1 million young women under 20—one out of every 10 American girls—become pregnant. More than 40% of our teenage girls will become pregnant before they reach their 20th birthday and those from minority backgrounds and those living in poverty are more likely to become pregnant than others. Approximately half of these young women carry the pregnancy to term, resulting in a live birth. According to the Alan Guttmacher Institute, fewer than 10% of teenagers who give birth choose adoption for their children, so the vast majority of these young parents keep their children and assume parental responsibilities. Unfortunately, most teenage mothers have not completed their high school education, nor do they have the financial resources or family support to provide adequately [for] a nurturing environment for their offspring. There is no simple solution or answer to the situation of adolescent pregnancy, yet educational leaders are in a pivotal position to provide direction as to how schools and communities will meet the needs of pregnant and parenting teens and their children. Adolescent parents and their children fare better in communities where school leaders have taken a proactive lead in providing comprehensive, special programs to meet their unique needs.

Treatment of Teen Mothers Has Improved Since the 1960s

Until the late 1960s, the almost universal response to teen pregnancy in public schools was expulsion, unless the pregnant teen was secretly sent to a maternity home. Unwed adolescent mothers were scorned, punished, shamed, and blamed. Title IX of the Federal Education Amendments of 1972 stopped schools from forcing pregnant teens to drop out. Title IX prohibits the expulsion or exclusion of students from any program, course, or extracurricular activities solely on the basis of pregnancy or parenthood, regardless of marital status. Beyond satisfying the legal obligation to educate these students, school districts were encouraged to develop policies and programming to meet the unique needs of pregnant and parenting teenagers so that they could complete their education, become productive members of their communities, and lessen the likelihood of their economic dependence on society. By 1973, more than 200 local school systems in the United States had created programs to encourage pregnant school-age girls and young mothers to continue their education, obtain prenatal care, and engage in group counseling to help solve problems that either may have led to or been caused by the pregnancy. Most of these programs offered young mothers a regular educational program in a special setting.

Today, nearly 30 years later, one might imagine that most U.S. school systems would have programs and services specifically for educating pregnant teens. However, that is not the case. The predominant attitude in schools across the country, when faced with pregnant and parenting teenagers, has been to ignore the situation, assuming that pregnant students will drop out. Some are concerned that the presence of student parents in the classroom will convey the wrong impression to non-pregnant students, namely that the school and society accept and condone teen parenthood. Others have denied that the problem exists in their district. Thanks to Title IX teen mothers now have the right to stay in school, but few have the financial ability or support systems to solve the child care and transportation problems that keep them from attending. Unfortunately, Title IX does not mandate that programs be created to meet their special needs, so many schools continue to ignore the problem of adolescent pregnancy or pretend it doesn't exist.

Schools Are the Logical Place to Educate Teen Parents

Schools are the most logical catalyst for generating a proactive approach to adolescent pregnancy. No other social institution has sufficient access to teenagers to have the necessary impact. Schools are capable of setting up networks and helping families

Public Services to Teen Mothers Can Be Costly

AGE	WIC	Food Stamps	Medicaid Prenatal/ Delivery/Infant	Public Assistance	Total
All (teenagers and 20–24 years old)	$277	$291	$4,777	$113	$5,458
% Users	79.80%	22.29%	68.30%	13.08%	47.81%
All teenagers (<20 years old)	$322	$357	$5,555	$117	$6,720
% Users	85.21%	24.74%	72.64%	17.54%	66.63%
<16 years old	$398	$545	$5,327		$6,610
% Users	96.89%	22.41%	76.39%	*	52.25%
16–17 years old	$341	$355	$5,787	$126	$6,610
% Users	82.34%	22.41%	71.67%	32.58%	52.25%
18–19 years old	$309	$352	$5,442	$115	$6,219
% Users	77.57%	22.92%	70.24%	4.26%	43.75%
20–24 years old	$247	$248	$4,269	$111	$4,875
% Users	64.11%	15.45%	55.70%	3.70%	34.74%

Based on data from Alabama, Alaska, Florida, Maine, North Carolina, New York (excludes New York City), Oklahoma, South Carolina, Washington, and West Virginia.

*Number of teenagers <16 years old was too small in eight of ten study states.

Taken from: E. Kathleen Adams et al., "The Costs of Public Services for Teenage Mothers Post–Welfare Reform: A Ten-State Study," *Journal of Health Care Finance*, Spring 2009, p. 50.

deal with the situation, all while meeting the students' educational needs. Many students also have important relationships with their teachers or other school staff. Schools can create a safe environment where young people can explore questions of sexuality in a responsible manner. Students can learn to understand the consequences of their choices rather than acting according to messages from peers or the media. Schools can develop policies and programs to address both primary prevention, to result in fewer pregnant teenagers, and secondary prevention, to result in healthier infants, fewer school dropouts, and more teenage parents graduating from high school and acquiring jobs that enable them to support their new families.

The consequences of teenage pregnancy are both far-reaching and cyclical, with implications for the education, health, and well-being of both the young parents and their offspring. Educational consequences of teenage pregnancy and parenting are twofold: young mothers and fathers are at high risk of not gaining the educational skills necessary to be self-supporting, economically productive citizens, and their children often enter the educational system with economic and developmental disadvantages. Youth with poor basic skills, regardless of race or ethnicity, are more than three times as likely to be teen parents as are students with average or better basic skills. Pregnancy and parenting are the number one reason females cite for dropping out of school. Teen parents who drop out of school are at an increased risk of entering a cycle of welfare dependency.

Providing Special Programs Increases Graduation Rates

Providing special programs for teenage mothers and their children dramatically increases high school graduation rates for this population of students. In a comprehensive school-based program for teenage mothers and their children in Plainfield, New Jersey, [researchers D. Fuscaldo Dellano et al. report] "a significantly higher percentage of the program mothers graduated from high school (84%) than did comparison mothers (41%)." School staff members at this same high school believe the program helped prevent school dropout among teen mothers. Similar success among teen parenting programs in promoting school completion was found in other studies.

Decision makers at all levels need to be aware of the true numbers, circumstances, and needs of parenting adolescents within their community and within individual systems. Adolescent parents and their children are a highly vulnerable population, yet they are not highly visible within most public systems. In most communities, the total number of parenting teens or of the young children of teen parents is not known. Very often the number of parenting teens in a community is assumed to be the number of teen births in a given year. However, in fact, it is several times that number when you factor in young mothers who gave birth in earlier years and are still teenagers. Accurate data are needed to raise awareness and assist decision makers in addressing needs in the most effective manner.

Generally, teen parents have few natural advocates. Parents are reluctant to be vocal about demanding services for their pregnant daughters. The school nurse may try to be an advocate, but school nurses may not be school employees, so they may not have much authority. Because most student record systems generally do not identify parenting students, teen parents can get lost within the general student population. Furthermore, adolescent pregnancy frequently goes unrecognized when students drop out of school without giving reasons. These young people may not have access to available services because of their own intimidation or lack of knowledge. Additionally, a gap between the number of parenting teens in the community and those known to be enrolled in public school programs creates the need for identification and outreach.

Children of Teen Parents Also Need Assistance

Advocacy is even more necessary for the young children of adolescent mothers, because the focus of the school building staff is on students at the secondary level (the mothers), not on school readiness for the primary grade students (their children). One particularly startling statistic from the past 2 decades should bring this issue to the attention of all educational leaders: In the state of California [researchers N. Compton et al. report that] "annually, a minimum of 2,118 kindergarten classes costing almost $276 million will be needed to serve only the children born to teen mothers." We must see to it that today's and tomorrow's children grow into productive and compassionate adults, because the security of all of us will eventually come to rest on their shoulders.

Pregnant and parenting teens face significant barriers to academic achievement, largely because traditional school programs often conflict with the demands of pregnancy and child rearing. The younger the single-parent mother, the less likely she is to finish high school. [According to researcher M. Gallagher,] "Less than half of teens who

During a pregnancy and parenting class at the John Hope Education Center in Indianapolis, a teacher instructs a pregnant student on what to expect when giving birth. The center specializes in counseling students who are at risk of failing school or dropping out.

become pregnant between 13 and 15 graduate from high school." While the dominant trend in school policies affecting pregnant and parenting students has been what is called "mainstreaming," this may not meet the unique needs of this population. According to one national study, teen mothers who attended vocational programs that serve as special programs for pregnant teens were almost twice as likely as similar teen mothers in regular schools to graduate. Some characteristics of effective alternative programs for pregnant and parenting teens include small class sizes, nurturance, personalized guidance, and mentoring. Teen mothers need what all teens need, only more so; close adult attention, guidance, and support, which is often not available for pregnant girls in regular schools. The most poorly performing students in regular schools are often the ones who reap the greatest benefits from alternative schools or specialized programs. Researchers Nancy Apfel and Victoria Seitz conducted a 20-year study of the McCabe School in New Haven, Connecticut, an alternative school for pregnant students and their children. This separate school functioned as an excellent dropout prevention program for students who had been 'D' and 'F' students prior to their pregnancy. The longer a pregnant girl attended McCabe, the better she did. Students at high scholastic risk appear to require a specialized school program. . . .

Teen Parenting Impacts Everyone

Adolescent parenting impacts society as a whole. Increases in welfare, food stamps, and medical care expenses cost U.S. taxpayers an estimated $6.9 billion each year, a significant portion of the gross annual cost estimated at $34 billion. In addition, educational leaders need to keep in mind that the percentage of American adolescents who are sexually active has increased significantly in recent years. Currently, 56% of girls and 73% of boys have had sexual intercourse before 18 years of age. To reduce the number of pregnant and parenting teens who drop out, schools can introduce and enforce policies and practices that encourage and create ways for pregnant and parenting teens to remain in school and complete their high school education, while still complying with Title IX. . . .

For the past several decades, schools have come to play a greatly expanded role in our children's lives. We now look to the schools to teach not only academics but also career education, character education, health education, driver education, and vocational education. This represents a change from the family to the school as the primary educational and socializing institution, which necessitates that educational leaders provide direction as to how schools and communities will meet the needs of pregnant and parenting teens and their children. . . . Adolescent parents and their children, in addition to the whole community, will benefit immensely when comprehensive, special programs are provided to meet their unique needs.

TEN

TV Teen Parenting Shows Are Realistic

Jennifer Grant

Jennifer Grant writes for the *Chicago Tribune* and *Christianity Today*. She has also written a book about adopting her own daughter called *Love You More: The Divine Surprise of Adopting My Daughter*, published in 2011 by Thomas Nelson. In this viewpoint, she writes about the MTV shows *16 and Pregnant* and *Teen Mom*. Grant believes that these shows do present a realistic picture of teen parenting because they show the abusive and painful relationships the teens have with their families and with each other, and the difficult decisions that teen parents face. She especially applauds two teen parents on the *Teen Mom* show, Catelynn and Tyler, who made the decision to give their daughter, Carly, up for adoption to give her a chance for a better life.

MTV may not go down in history as the network that best encouraged young viewers to make wise choices and live responsibly. But two of its most popular shows, *16 and Pregnant* and its *Teen Mom* spinoffs, just might be promoting—ironically and unintentionally—a few moral lessons after all.

You're not likely to hear MTV preaching abstinence any time soon; "safe sex" and/or "responsible sex" are more likely the network's unwritten mantras. But by letting the cameras capture the gritty and difficult consequences of teen pregnancy

Jennifer Grant, "Pregnant Pause: MTV's 'Teen Mom' Might Be Sending an Abstinence Message After All," from *Christianity Today*, January 11, 2011. Reproduced by permission of the author.

and motherhood, these popular reality TV shows are certainly delivering a message. But is it a good one? Depends who you ask.

Bristol Palin—a teen mom herself and a fellow reality show star—insists that *Teen Mom* doesn't "glamorize teen pregnancy" but illustrates "how difficult it really is." The National Campaign to Prevent Teen Pregnancy and the Henry J. Kaiser Family Foundation praise the show. But other critics, including the Parents Television Council, say *Teen Mom* normalizes, or even romanticizes, teen pregnancy and parenthood.

While the pundits dispute its merits, the world watches. *Teen Mom* attracted close to three million viewers every week and six million for the season finale. *Teen Mom 2*, with an all-new cast (featuring the girls from Season Two of *16 and Pregnant*), expects similarly high ratings. The shows' producers don't have to look very hard for subjects: According to the Centers for Disease Control, 435,000 infants were born to teenaged mothers in the U.S. in 2008.

Tabloid Fodder, Poignant Scenes

Before the two seasons of *Teen Mom*, Amber Portwood, Catelynn Lowell, Farrah Abraham, and Maci Bookout composed the cast of *16 and Pregnant*. Since then, their faces and the intimate (and sometimes banal) details of their lives have been tabloid fodder with titillating headlines: "Teen Mom Slapped with Domestic Violence Charges!" "Teen Moms Under the Knife!" "Teen Mom: 'I'm broke!'" (The stories don't mention that the young women reportedly received compensation of $65,000 last season.)

Viewers are stunned by scenes of Amber physically abusing Gary Shirley, the father of her baby. (Portwood is currently under investigation for these attacks and, in November [2010], temporarily lost custody of her daughter.) We are shocked by the snapshots of Farrah's split lip, an injury suffered at the hand of her mother. We wince at the expletives that the teen moms, their boyfriends, and their parents exchange.

And we weep as Catelynn and Tyler Baltierra—the father of her baby, Carly—stand on a suburban sidewalk and lovingly place

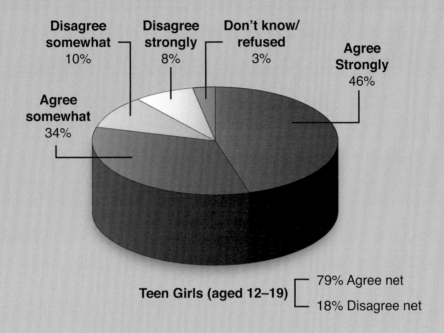

Media's Influence on Teen Pregnancy

Question:
How much do you agree or disagree with the following statement:

"When a TV show or character I like deals with teen pregnancy, it makes me think more about my own risk of getting pregnant / causing a pregnancy and how to avoid it."

Disagree somewhat 10%

Disagree strongly 8%

Don't know/ refused 3%

Agree Strongly 46%

Agree somewhat 34%

Teen Girls (aged 12–19)

79% Agree net

18% Disagree net

Taken from: The National Campaign to Prevent Pregnancy, *Fast Facts: Does the Media Glamorize Teen Pregnancy? New Polling Data on What Teens Think*, October 2010, p. 2. www.thenationalcampaign.org.

Carly into her adoptive parents' arms, who then drive away in their luxury SUV. In later episodes, we meet Carly as an older baby and toddler. She is thriving and loved.

When Catelynn and Tyler place baby Carly with her new family, the young parents—as well as viewers—feel a sense of relief. During the pregnancy, they had lived with their parents—a strange situation in itself. Tyler's father, Butch, and Catelynn's mother, April, met and married after the two teenagers began

In Decembeer 2010, MTV's Teen Mom *reality star Amber Portwood leaves the county jail in Madison, Indiana, after posting bond on felony battery and neglect charges stemming from a previously aired episode in which she was seen assaulting her child's father.*

dating. Butch is a cocaine addict who had been incarcerated for much of Tyler's childhood; April verbally abuses her daughter. At one point, Tyler told his father that Carly "deserves much better than this." At another, he said, "How am I supposed to raise a kid when I'm a kid myself? Can you imagine how screwed up this kid would be?"

Powerful words, effective social commentary—and, for many, good advice. Teen viewers can't help but hear the words as wise counsel from a peer. And it's probably better advice than the teens on these shows are getting from adults. The closest most of them get in solid "grown-up advice" comes from Dr. Drew Pinsky in post-show interviews and filmed therapy sessions. An addiction specialist whose TV credits include *Celebrity Rehab with Dr. Drew* and *Sex Rehab with Dr. Drew*, Pinsky provides common sense advice, sprinkled with occasional factoids like this: "Sixty percent of sexually active kids say they wished they had waited longer." Pinsky refers viewers to the show's website for more information, but they won't find much on abstinence there. One of the organizations listed, Stayteen.org (from the National Campaign to Prevent Teen and Unplanned Pregnancy), tells teens "it's okay not to have sex," and to "Stay silly. Stay random. Life is full of positives. Don't let a pregnancy test be one of them."

Adoption Is Shown as a Positive Option

Happily, two of the teen parents, Catelynn and Tyler, did have access to a wise adult—Dawn Baker, supervisor of the Pregnancy Counseling and Infant Adoption Programs at Bethany Christian Services in Michigan. Count her among the shows' supporters.

"I believe that *16 and Pregnant* does a terrific job of showing the reality of teen pregnancy and the hurdles teens face in parenting," Baker tells [*Christianity Today*]. "It does not glorify the process in any way but gives an accurate accounting of the personal struggles and the difficult adult decisions that teens are faced with when they encounter an unplanned pregnancy. *16 and Pregnant* and *Teen Mom* have both honored the process of adoption."

For better and worse, *Teen Mom* provides valuable—if not embellished—lessons about the consequences of unplanned pregnancy as well as insights into the legacy of adults repeating, with their own children, the patterns of abuse they suffered. But with Catelynn, Tyler, and Carly, we get a glimpse of something redemptive. When the teen parents make the brave choice to place their baby for adoption, the cycle of abuse is broken and viewers get a hint of what adoption into God's family is like.

ELEVEN

TV Teen Parenting Shows Ignore Pregnancy Prevention

Liz Goodwin

> Liz Goodwin is an assistant editor at the news website the
> Daily Beast. In this viewpoint, she discusses MTV's reality
> show *Teen Mom* and a number of other television shows
> that depict pregnant teens and teen parents. Goodwin
> says that *Teen Mom* glorifies teen pregnancy by taking
> high school girls who should not have gotten pregnant
> in the first place and making them into television stars.
> She complains that the shows do not talk about how to
> prevent pregnancy or how to terminate an unwanted preg-
> nancy by abortion, both of which she considers important
> for teens to know.

Last week [January 2010] a new report delivered depressing news: After 15 years of decline, the teen pregnancy rate rose three percent among 15 to 19 year olds. The report, released by the Guttmacher Institute, did not speculate as to why this might be the case, only gesturing at other studies that suggest shift- ing demographics and the push for abstinence-only education in public schools during the [George W.] Bush years as possible causes. (President [Barack] Obama has since abolished funding for abstinence-only education, but the Senate could fund it again as part of health-care reform.)

"The United States has levels of pregnancy that are two to four times higher than European nations," Heather Boonstra, senior public policy associate at the Guttmacher Institute, told The Daily Beast, arguing that an influx of images of teen pregnancy in the media, coupled with a lack of information about sex and contraceptives have created a "perfect storm of teen pregnancy."

"It makes you scratch your head and think, why are our rates so high?" she said. "There's a glorification of having children [in our culture]."

Television Shows About Pregnant Teenagers Are Popular

Indeed, it seems American viewers cannot get enough of pregnant teenagers: Real-life teen mom Bristol Palin recently appeared on *Oprah* with her mother, endorsing abstinence until marriage to her flummoxed host. (Sarah Palin awkwardly quipped, "Does that mean you're going to marry pretty young?") In a fictional example on the popular show *Glee*, a cheerleader and leader of the abstinence club, Quinn, gets pregnant and arranges an adoption with the crazed wife of her glee club coach. *The Secret Life of the American Teenager, Private Practice,* and *Friday Night Lights* all featured teen characters getting pregnant in recent episodes. And Anna North at Jezebel points out that the wild success of *The Pregnancy Pact*, a new Lifetime movie about a semi-fictional pact among Massachusetts high school girls to get pregnant before graduation, shows that we as a culture "are fascinated with teen pregnancy—just not with teaching kids real ways to avoid it." *The Pregnancy Pact* was the top-rated movie on ad-supported cable since 1998 among women 18 to 34.

Perhaps the slickest example of the trend is the MTV reality show *Teen Mom*, billed as an unvarnished look at the consequences of teen pregnancy, and sponsored by the Campaign to Prevent Teen and Unplanned Pregnancy. The show follows the lives of four teenagers who have babies, and the main characters grapple with real problems as the cameras roll.

"Oh, haven't you heard? Babies are "out," cartoon by Gareth Cowlin. www.CartoonStock.com.

"I just want Bentley to have a dad," says *Teen Mom* star Maci, tearing up in front of friends who ask about her relationship to her unhelpful boyfriend, Ryan. Another teen mom, Amber, sobs in front of a career counselor as she realizes she doesn't have time to get her GED [high school diploma equivalent] now that she's working and living on her own with her baby. Catelynn, who gave her baby up for adoption, begins to cry when she sees photos of her six-month-old. "What do we say about that?" asks the slightly overbearing representative at the adoption clinic.

"It's not goodbye, it's see you later," Catelynn obediently repeats, tears still streaming down her face.

Making Teen Moms into Television Stars

Sure, *Teen Mom* depicts real young women—women who know they shouldn't have gotten pregnant in high school with their deadbeat [nonsupporting] (or even non-deadbeat) boyfriends. But either way, these girls are the stars of a popular reality show, produced by the same person who was behind the mega-hit, glossy reality series *Laguna Beach*. Like *Laguna Beach*, *Teen Mom* is highly stylized—there's a soundtrack, girly animation that flashes up when the show switches from one teen mom to the next, voiceovers, and uplifting narrative arcs punctuated by moments of emotional clarity from the show's stars.

For example, by the end of the season, Farrah, the spoiled 18-year-old co-raising her daughter with her controlling mom, decides to stop fighting and begin appreciating her mother's help, saying in a voice-over that her mom is her "partner" in raising her daughter. It's possible that Farrah actually did feel completely at peace with her mother just in time for the show's season finale, but only the week before the show aired, reports surfaced that Farrah's mom had been arrested for assaulting her, belying the show's neat ending.

Neglecting to Teach Pregnancy Prevention

But even more troubling is that the new teen pregnancy shows aren't familiarizing viewers with ways to actually prevent pregnancy, or terminate an unwanted one—depictions of abortion have always been taboo on American television in the U.S. In real life, though, girls talk about birth control, condoms, and even abortion. On TV, the message is simply, *It's horrible to get pregnant as a teen*. By ignoring the prevention aspect, at best they are obscuring contraception, and at worst, making it seem weird or taboo.

Bill Albert, chief program officer at The National Campaign to Prevent Teen and Unplanned Pregnancy, an organization that has partnered with *Teen Mom* and other shows, thinks any attention to the issue is a good thing. "I've heard people's criticism that these shows might glamorize pregnancy—I don't understand that," he

MTV's Teen Mom *reality star Maci Bookout (far left) is one of four pregnant teens featured on the show. Critics say the show addresses neither pregnancy prevention nor information on terminating unwanted pregnancies.*

said. "Our view is that it shows that being a mother as a teenager is, to say the very least, challenging. Let's set aside whether we think these portrayals are good bad or indifferent. In our point of view it is a net gain to get teens talking about teen pregnancy—the good, the bad or the ugly."

Albert admitted he wishes there were more depictions of contraceptive use in television shows and movies, and that if there were a show that depicted an abortion, his organization would consider partnering with it. (The group, though, does not work with *Friday Night Lights*, which featured an abortion this season.)

"If we avoid pregnancy in the first place everybody is better off," he said. That may be true, but it's unclear how a parade of pregnant teenagers on television is going to further that goal.

What You Should Know About Teen Parenting

Birth Rates for Teen Mothers

The Centers for Disease Control and Prevention's National Center for Health Statistics reports that:

- the birth rate for US teenagers fell 6 percent in 2009, the lowest level recorded in nearly seven decades of tracking teenage childbearing (since 1940);
- the rate in 2009 was 39.1 births per thousand teenagers fifteen to nineteen years old, down from 41.5 in 2008 and 8 percent lower than in 2007; and
- the rate for 2009 was 37 percent lower than in 1991.

According to the Guttmacher Institute:

- Ten percent of all US births are to girls aged nineteen or younger;
- most births to teen mothers are first births;
- the share of births to teen mothers that are not married rose from 79 percent in 2000 to 87 percent in 2008, yet, over the last several decades the share of all nonmarital births that are to teenagers has been declining—from 52 percent in 1975 to 22 percent in 2008;
- teen fatherhood rates vary considerably by race—in 2006, the rate among black males aged fifteen to nineteen who became fathers (thirty-four per thousand) was more than twice that among whites (fifteen per thousand); and

- the rate of teen fatherhood declined 25 percent between 1990 and 2006; a decline that was far more substantial among blacks than among whites.

Ethnicity is a factor in teen pregnancy and birth rates. Rates have declined dramatically for black teens but have declined much more slowly for Latina teens.

The National Campaign to Prevent Teen and Unplanned Pregnancy reports that:
- 52 percent of Latina teens get pregnant at least once before age twenty—nearly twice the national average;
- Latinas have the highest teen pregnancy rate *and* teen birth rate of any major ethnic/racial minority in the country;
- Latina teen birth rates have declined about half as fast as non-Hispanic white and non-Hispanic black teen birth rates;
- 50 percent of black teen girls get pregnant at least once before age twenty—nearly twice the national average; and
- despite an increase between 2005 and 2006, the pregnancy rates among black teen girls have declined dramatically over the past fifteen years.

According to Planned Parenthood:
- The US teenage birth rate is the highest among the most developed countries in the world—more than two and a half times as high as Australia, nearly three times as high as Canada, nearly four times as high as Germany, nearly five and a half times as high as France, nearly seven and a half times as high as Japan, and nearly nine times as high as the Netherlands.
- Reasons for the lower rates of teenage childbearing in these other countries include:
  - mandatory, medically accurate sexuality education programs that provide comprehensive information and encourage teens to make responsible choices;
  - easy access to contraception and other forms of reproductive health care, including abortion;

- social acceptance of adolescent sexual expression as normal and healthy;
- straightforward public health media campaigns; and
- government support for the right of teens to accurate information and confidential services.

Public Costs of Teen Childbearing

Public funding is necessary to support many teen mothers and their children. According to a fact sheet by the National Campaign to Prevent Teen and Unplanned Pregnancy:

- The cost to taxpayers (federal, state, and local) of teen childbearing in the United States in 2004 was $9.1 billion, including:
  - $1.9 billion in increased public sector health care costs,
  - $2.3 billion in increased child welfare costs,
  - $2.1 billion in increased costs of incarceration, and
  - $2.9 billion in lost revenue due to lower taxes paid by the children of teen mothers over their own adult lifetimes as a result of lower education and earnings;
- state-by-state analysis of the costs of teen childbearing in 2004 ranged from a high of $1 billion in Texas to a low of $12 million in Vermont.

Teen Parents Often Delay Their Own Development

Child Trends reports that

- teen mothers have lower high school diploma attainment than those who did not have a teen birth;
- young women who had been teen mothers were less likely than other young women to earn a high school diploma by the age of twenty-two;
- one in three young women (34 percent) who had been teen mothers earned *neither* a high school diploma nor a GED by age twenty-two, compared with only 6 percent of young women who had not had a teen birth;
- younger teen mothers are less likely than older teen mothers to earn a diploma;

- young women who gave birth before the age of eighteen were far less likely than were those who gave birth between the ages of eighteen and nineteen to earn a high school diploma; and
- black teen mothers are more likely than Hispanic or white teen mothers to earn a diploma/GED by age twenty-two.

Planned Parenthood reports that in general, teenage mothers do not fare as well as their peers who delay childbearing because
- their family incomes are lower,
- they are more likely to be poor and receive public assistance,
- they are less educated,
- they are less likely to be married, and
- their children lag in standards of early development.

Teen fathers also have additional challenges. According to Healthy Teen Network:
- Despite the stereotypes, there is increasing evidence that teen fathers want to be (and are) involved with their children, though this involvement may not always include financial support;
- teen fatherhood appears to be associated with negative consequences, both for the father and child, that are similar to those observed among teen mothers;
- these consequences include reduced educational attainment, greater financial hardship, and less stable marriage patterns for the teen parent, along with poorer health, educational, and behavioral outcomes among children born to teen parents;
- young fathers are more likely to have economic and employment challenges and are more often economically disadvantaged than adult fathers;
- young fathers face premature role transition, which causes added stress to their lives because they are expected to mediate both the transition to parenthood and the tasks of adolescent development.

Having a Teen Mother or Father Affects Children

Planned Parenthood reports that

- because one-third of pregnant teens do not receive adequate prenatal care, their babies are 23 percent more likely to be low birth weight, to have childhood health problems, and to be hospitalized than those born to older mothers; and that
- in 2004, the infant mortality rate for children born to teen mothers was significantly higher than the national infant mortality rate.

According to the National Center for Chronic Disease Prevention and Health Promotion, Division of Reproductive Health, children who are born to teen mothers experience a wide range of problems, including being more likely to

- have fewer skills and be less prepared to learn when they enter kindergarten,
- have behavioral problems and chronic medical conditions,
- rely more heavily on publicly funded health care,
- be incarcerated at some time during adolescence,
- drop out of high school,
- give birth as a teenager,
- be unemployed or underemployed as a young adult.

What You Should Do About Teen Parenting

Gather Information

The first step in grappling with any complex and controversial issue is to be informed about it. Gather as much information as you can from a variety of sources. The essays in this book provide an excellent starting point, representing a variety of viewpoints and approaches to the topic. Your school or local library will be another source of useful information; look there for relevant books, magazines, and encyclopedia entries. The Bibliography and Organizations to Contact sections of this book will give you useful starting points in gathering additional information. Visit the websites of the organizations listed in the Organizations to Contact section to learn more. Do an Internet search for "teen parenting" to find more organizations. You will also find a variety of opinions about teen parenting on television shows and in popular magazines.

Identify the Issues Involved

Once you have gathered your information, review it methodically to discover the key issues involved. When a teen becomes pregnant and the decision is made to become a parent, the issues then revolve around balancing the needs of the child with the needs of the teen parent, who is not quite an adult her- or himself. Consider the challenges teen parents face as they continue to grow up, try to get an education, and look for a job while also caring for a new infant. Consider also the challenges the child may face by having a teen parent or parents. What are the challenges? How can they be addressed? How is life different for a teen who is a parent compared with a teen who is not? What are the differences and similarities between the life of a celebrity teen parent and a noncelebrity teen parent? What are the positive aspects of being a teen parent?

Evaluate Your Information Sources

As you learn about a topic, make sure to evaluate the sources of the information you have discovered. Authors always speak from their own perspective, which influences the way they perceive a subject and how they present information.

Consider each author's experience and background. Is he or she a teen parent? Or the child of a teen parent? Or the parent of a teen parent? Has he or she done research on the subject and gathered statistics? Someone with a personal perspective has a very different point of view from someone who has studied the issue at a distance. Both can be useful, but it is important to recognize what the author bases his or her opinion on. For example, someone who has been a teen parent could report that she is very happy with the way her life turned out. Someone else could report from an academic perspective that a certain percentage of teen parents have a more difficult life than teens who are not parents. Both points of view are valid. They just present different perspectives.

Examine Your Own Perspective

Consider your own beliefs, feelings, and biases on this issue. Before you began studying, did you have an opinion about teen parenting? If so, what influenced you to have this opinion—friends, family, personal experience, something you read or heard in the media? Be careful to acknowledge your own viewpoint and be willing to learn about other sides of the issue. Make sure to study and honestly consider opinions that are different from yours. Do they make some points that might convince you to change your mind? Do they raise more questions that you need to think about? Or does looking at other viewpoints more solidly convince you of your own initial perspective?

Form Your Own Opinion

Once you have gathered and organized information, identified the issues involved, and examined your own perspective, you will be ready to form an opinion on teen parenting and to advocate for that position in debates and discussions. You may decide that the challenges faced by teen parents and the children of teen parents are too difficult and that teens should choose not to become parents. Or you may decide that the joys of becoming a parent outweigh the challenges and that more teens should choose to become parents. These are just a couple of the opinions that you might form after learning more about this issue. Whatever position you take, be prepared to explain it clearly on the basis of evidence and well-thought-out opinions.

Take Action

Once you have developed your position on teen parenting, you can consider turning your beliefs into action. Advocating your position in discussions and debates is one place to start. You also might want to join an organization that shares your beliefs about teen parenting—see the Organizations to Contact section of this book for some starting points. These organizations offer ways that you can support teen parents or advocate to discourage teens from becoming parents.

ORGANIZATIONS TO CONTACT

The editors have compiled the following list of organizations concerned with the issues debated in this book. The descriptions are derived from materials provided by the organizations. All have publications or information available for interested readers. The list was compiled on the date of publication of the present volume; the information provided here may change. Be aware that many organizations take several weeks or longer to respond to inquiries, so allow as much time as possible for the receipt of requested materials.

Center for Family Connections (CFFC)
350 Cambridge St., Cambridge, MA 02141
(617) 547-0909 • fax: (617) 497-5952
e-mail: cffc@kinnect.org • website: www.kinnect.org

The goal of the Center for Family Connections is to serve individuals and families touched by adoption, foster care, kinship, and guardianship, as well as other complex family issues, and to serve the people with whom they are connected by offering training, education, consultation, advocacy, and clinical treatment. CFFC publishes the *Kids Newsletter*.

Centers for Disease Control and Prevention (CDC)
1600 Clifton Rd., Atlanta, GA 30333
(800) 232-4636 • e-mail: cdcinfo@cdc.gov
website: www.cdc.gov/teenpregnancy

The CDC is one of the major operating components of the Department of Health and Human Services. CDC's mission is to collaborate to create the expertise, information, and tools that people and communities need to protect their health—through health promotion; prevention of disease, injury, and disability; and preparedness for new health threats. A portion of the organization's website is devoted to teen pregnancy and reproductive health.

Child Welfare League of America (CWLA)

1726 M St. NW, Suite 500, Washington, DC 20036
(202) 688-4200 • fax: (202) 833-1689
website: www.cwla.org

CWLA is a coalition of private and public agencies that has been serving vulnerable children and families since 1920. The organization's vision is that every child will grow up in a safe, loving, and stable family. Publications and resources on teen parenting are included on its website.

Family and Youth Services Bureau (FYSB)

National Clearinghouse on Families and Youth
PO Box 13505, Silver Spring, MD 20911-3505
(301) 608-8098 • fax: (301) 608-8721
e-mail: ncfy@acf.hhs.gov • website: www.acf.hhs.gov/programs/fysb

The Family and Youth Services Bureau is part of the Administration for Children and Families of the US Department of Health and Human Services. The mission of FYSB is to provide national leadership on youth and family issues. The organization's Teen Pregnancy Prevention Program provides fact sheets and other information on teen pregnancy and teen parents.

Guttmacher Institute

125 Maiden Ln., 7th floor, New York, NY 10038
(212) 248-1111 • fax: (212) 248-1951
website: www.guttmacher.org

The Guttmacher Institute exists to advance sexual and reproductive health in the United States and worldwide through an interrelated program of social science research, policy analysis, and public education designed to generate new ideas, encourage enlightened public debate, and promote sound policy and program development. The institute produces a wide range of resources on topics pertaining to sexual and reproductive health. In 2009, Guttmacher was designated an official Collaborating Center for Reproductive Health by the World Health Organization (WHO) and the WHO's regional office, the Pan American Health

Organization. The Guttmacher Institute's website includes a section on adolescents that offers fact sheets, articles, and research reports.

Healthy Teen Network
1501 Saint Paul St., Suite 124, Baltimore, MD 21202
(410) 685-0410 • fax: (410) 685-0481
website: www.healthyteennetwork.org

The Healthy Teen Network is a national organization focused on adolescent health and well-being with an emphasis on teen pregnancy prevention, teen pregnancy, and teen parenting. The network builds capacity among professionals and organizations through education, advocacy, and networking so that these can assist all adolescents and young adults, including teen parents, to have access to the services and education that allow them to make responsible choices about childbearing and family formation, and so that they are supported and empowered to lead healthy sexual, reproductive, and family lives. The organization's website includes a number of publications on teen pregnancy and parenting

The National Campaign to Prevent Teen and Unplanned Pregnancy
1776 Massachusetts Ave. NW, Suite 200, Washington, DC 20036
(202) 478-8500 • fax: (202) 478-8588
website: www.thenationalcampaign.org

The National Campaign to Prevent Teen and Unplanned Pregnancy seeks to improve the lives and future prospects of children and families and, in particular, to help ensure that children are born into stable, two-parent families that are committed to and ready for the demanding task of raising the next generation. Its main goal is to prevent teen pregnancy and unplanned pregnancy among single, young adults by supporting a combination of responsible values and behavior by both men and women and responsible policies in both the public and private sectors. The organization's website has national and state data on teen pregnancy and childbirth and a downloadable version of its publication *With One Voice: America's Adults and Teens Sound Off About Teen Pregnancy.* It also sponsors stayteen.org, a website specifically for teens that helps teens enjoy their teen years and avoid the responsibilities that come with too-early pregnancy and parenting.

National Fatherhood Initiative (NFI)

20410 Observation Dr., Suite 107, Germantown, MD 20876
(301) 948-0599 • fax: (301) 948-4325
e-mail: info@fatherhood.org
website: http://fatherhood.org; www.fathersource.org

National Fatherhood Initiative's mission is to improve the well-being of children by increasing the proportion of children growing up with involved, responsible, and committed fathers. The organization works with local, state, and national organizations across the country to reach fathers at their point of need with skill-building resources to help them be the best dads they can be. FatherSOURCE, the Fatherhood Resource Center, is the online hub of NFI's efforts. Resources are available through www.father source.org.

Planned Parenthood Federation of America (PPFA)

434 W. Thirty-Third St., New York, NY 10001
(212) 541-7800 • fax: (212) 245-1845
website: www.plannedparenthood.org

Planned Parenthood Federation of America is a health care provider, educator, advocate, and global partner helping similar organizations around the world. Planned Parenthood delivers vital health care services, sex education, and sexual health information to millions of women, men, and young people. Articles and fact sheets about a large variety of health topics can be found on its website.

Sex, Etc.
Center for Applied Psychology
Rutgers University, 41 Gordon Rd., Suite C, Piscataway, NJ 08854
(732) 445-7929 • fax: (732) 445-5333
e-mail: answered@rci.rutgers.edu • website: www.sexetc.org

Sex, Etc. is part of the Teen-to-Teen Sexuality Education Project developed by Answer, a national organization sponsored by Rutgers University, dedicated to providing and promoting comprehensive sexuality education to young people and the adults who teach them. The Sex, Etc., website provides information about sex and relationships, pregnancy, sexually transmited infections, birth control, sexual orientation, and more. The organization also publishes a printed magazine called *Sex, Etc.*

BIBLIOGRAPHY

Books

John G. Borkowski et al., *Risk and Resilience: Adolescent Mothers and Their Children Grow Up*. Mahwah, NJ: Lawrence Erlbaum, 2007.

Saul D. Hoffman and Rebecca A. Maynard, eds., *Kids Having Kids: Economic Costs & Social Consequences of Teen Pregnancy*. Washington, DC: Urban Institute Press, 2008.

Angelia M. Paschal, *Voices of African-American Teen Fathers: "I'm Doing What I Got to Do."* New York: Haworth, 2006.

Rae Simons, *Teen Parents*. Broomall, PA: Mason Crest, 2010.

Jack C. Westman, *Breaking the Adolescent Parent Cycle: Valuing Fatherhood and Motherhood*. Lanham, MD: University Press of America, 2009.

Robert Worth, *Frequently Asked Questions About Teen Fatherhood*. New York: Rosen, 2009.

Periodicals

Susan Black, "Children Having Children," *American School Board Journal*, May 2009.

Holly Corbett, "Don't Be a Teen Mom," *Seventeen*, April 2011.

Karen Fanning, "'My Job Is to Be a Mom': After the Birth of Her Son, a Teen Grows Up Quickly," *Scholastic Choices*, January 2009.

Sarah Kliff, "Teen Pregnancy, Hollywood Style," *Newsweek*, July 23, 2008.

Rachel Waugh, "My Mother, Myself: Old Questions Are Answered and New Ones Arise for Bryanna Nelson, Now Almost the Same Age as the Teen Mother Who Gave Her Up for Adoption," *Scholastic Choices*, September 2008.

Jennifer Westendorp, "The Best Job in the World: When You're a Teen, Babies Can Seem Gross. Until You Have One," *Today's Parent*, June 2010.

Sandra Sobieraj Westfall, "Bristol Palin, 'My Life Comes Second Now,'" *People Weekly*, June 1, 2009.

Kelly White, "When You Least Expect It," *GL*, March 2008.

Internet Sources

Karen Grigsby Bates, "MTV's 'Teen Mom' Makes for Teaching Moments," National Public Radio, August 10, 2010. www.npr .org/templates/story/story.php?storyId=128626258.

Neal Conan, "How Should Families Support Pregnant Teens?," *Talk of the Nation*, National Public Radio, September 18, 2008. www.npr.org/templates/story/story.php?storyId=94760964.

Ginnie Graham, "Teen Mothers Say They Lacked Sex Information," *Tulsa (OK) World*, September 26, 2010. www.tulsaworld.com/ news/article.aspx?subjectid=11&articleid=20100926_11_A9_ ULNSyn332195.

Guttmacher Institute, "Minors' Rights as Parents," *State Policies in Brief*, June 1, 2011. www.guttmacher.org/statecenter/spibs/ spib_MRP.pdf.

Healthy Teen Network, "The Unique Needs of Young Fathers," www .healthyteennetwork.org/vertical/Sites/%7BB4D0CC76-CF78- 4784-BA7C-5D0436F6040C%7D/uploads/%7B831934FA- 3A1B-42BB-8ED4-425528E23D5E%7D.PDF.

INDEX

A

Abortion/abortion rates, 47, 76
  among females aged 15–19 years, *13*
  as taboo on US television, 75
Abraham, Farrah, 68, 75
Adolescents
  parenthood and, 8–9
  percent sexually active, 66
Adoption, 12, 71
Alan Guttmacher Institute, 60, 72
Albert, Bill, 9, 11, 75–76
Aleman, Robert, 52, 58
Apfel, Nancy, 66
Apgar score, 34, 36

B

Bainbridge, Jane, 33
Baker, Dawn, 71
Baltierra, Tyler, 68–70, 71
Beers, Lee, 25
Birth control/contraception, 13, 75
Births/birth rates, teen, *13*, 27, 68
  by race/ethnicity, *16*
  by state, *57*
  states with highest, 54
  unplanned pregnancy and, *25, 50*

  in US *vs.* other nations, 53
  See also Preterm births
Bookout, Maci, 68, 74, 76
Boonstra, Heather, 73
Bracken, Maryann, 41
Bracken, Michael, 41
Bush, George W., 72

C

Casaclang, Sharlene, 56
Centers for Disease Control and Prevention (CDC), 68
Child Trends, 5, 54
Children
  cost of raising, 31–32
  teen fathers and, 33–37
  of teen parents, are disadvantaged, 11–12, 27–32
Compadre High School (AZ), 6
Compton, N., 64
Cortina, Betty, 14

D

Daly Melissa, 8
Dellano, D. Fuscaldo, 63
DeVito, Josephine, 5

F

Farber, Naomi, 38–39

PICTURE CREDITS